AARP Guide to
REVITALIZING YOUR HOME

AARP Guide to
REVITALIZING YOUR HOME

BEAUTIFUL LIVING FOR
THE SECOND HALF OF LIFE

REIMAGINE · REDESIGN · REMODEL

Rosemary Bakker

A Division of
Sterling Publishing Co., Inc.
New York / London

Editor
Deborah Morgenthal

Assistant Editor
Mark Bloom

Art Director
Kathleen Holmes

Junior Designer
Carol Morse

Photographer
Steve Mann

Photography Director
Dana Irwin

Cover Designer
Chris Bryant

AARP Books publishes a wide range of titles on health, personal finance, lifestyle, and other subjects that promise to enrich the lives of Americans 50+. For more information, go to www.aarp.org/books.

AARP, established in 1958, is a nonprofit, nonpartisan organization with more than 40 million members age 50 and older. The AARP name and logo are registered trademarks of AARP, used under license to Sterling Publishing Co., Inc.

The recommendations and opinions expressed herein are those of the author and do not necessarily reflect the views of AARP.

Library of Congress Cataloging-in-Publication Data

Bakker, Rosemary.
 AARP guide to revitalizing your home beautiful living for the second half of life reimagine, redesign, remodel / Rosemary Bakker. -- 1st ed.
    p. cm.
 Includes index.
  ISBN 978-1-60059-280-5 (pb-pbk. with flaps : alk. paper)
   1. Universal design. 2. Interior decoration. I. Title. II. Title: Redecorate, remodel & revitalize your home for the second half of your life.
  NA2545.A3B35 2009
  728.087--dc22

                                          2009032649

10 9 8 7 6 5 4 3 2 1

First Edition

Published by Lark Books, A Division of Sterling Publishing Co., Inc.
387 Park Avenue South, New York, NY 10016

Text © 2010, Rosemary Bakker

Photography © 2010, Lark Books, A Division of Sterling Publishing Co., Inc., unless otherwise specified

Distributed in Canada by Sterling Publishing,
c/o Canadian Manda Group, 165 Dufferin Street
Toronto, Ontario, Canada M6K 3H6

Distributed in the United Kingdom by GMC Distribution Services,
Castle Place, 166 High Street, Lewes, East Sussex, England BN7 1XU

Distributed in Australia by Capricorn Link (Australia) Pty Ltd.,
P.O. Box 704, Windsor, NSW 2756 Australia

If you have questions or comments about this book, please contact:

Lark Books
67 Broadway
Asheville, NC 28801
828-253-0467

Manufactured in China

ISBN 13: 978-1-60059-280-5

For information about custom editions, special sales, premium and corporate purchases, please contact Sterling Special Sales Department at 800-805-5489 or specialsales@sterlingpub.com.

For information about desk and examination copies available to college and university professors, requests must be submitted to academic@larkbooks.com. Our complete policy can be found at www.larkbooks.com.

Dedication

To my late mother, Arlene, and to my nephew Danny, for teaching me that it takes both an indomitable spirit and a universally designed environment to overcome disability and enjoy life.

Contents

Helpful Hints

Introduction

LIVING WELL IN YOUR HOME FOR THE SECOND HALF OF LIFE means discovering how that home can be beautiful at the same time it is safe, accessible, and comfortable. Throughout this book, I use the term "universal design" when discussing this goal. Perhaps you've heard the term "universal design," but you're not sure what it means and how it may be relevant to you. In its most general sense, universal design is an architectural and design concept intended to provide an accessible home environment for all people, regardless of their ability. In this book, universal design principles are expanded in their application and focus on a particular population.

Who Is This Book For?

How many of the scenarios below can you identify with?

• You're in your 50s, working, traveling, enjoying life. You own a home that you love, and you'd like to live there as long as possible. How do you decide whether or not that's a realistic goal? And if it is, what design changes do you need to make to create the safest, most accessible, and most comfortable home for the second half of your life?

• You're in your 60s, 70s, or beyond, still working, or retired, and you want to live on your own for as long as possible. Can the house you own now allow you to live independently, even if you become incapacitated in some way, while providing you with all the necessary comforts and security? Does your neighborhood offer the kinds of services and amenities you may need as you age?

• You're an adult who is starting to think about the safety of your aging parents, or you have a family member who's been diagnosed with a progressive disease. You're either a caregiver, or you can reasonably expect to be one in the near future. You're assessing the safety of your home from the standpoint of how well it will work for family members who have health and mobility issues.

If you checked off one or more of these scenarios, then this book is for you. As a member of the boomer generation myself, I know firsthand that the home that was comfortable and convenient in our younger years is often the very obstacle to wellness later in life.

Key ingredients to a long, healthy life are good friends, an active lifestyle, and a universally designed home that supports independence and safety.

Dr. Ethel Percy Andrus, AARP's founder, introduced the first "universal design" house to accommodate aging across the lifespan to President Dwight Eisenhower at the White House Conference on Aging in January 1961.

What Does This Book Offer?

I've been working in the field of gerontology and interior design for 15 years. Thirteen years ago, I published my first book on this subject, *Elder Design* (Penguin Books, 1997). Over the past decade, universal design has not only become more widely appreciated and practiced, but the concept itself has expanded beyond merely helping people survive in their environment. Now universal design incorporates principles to facilitate the physical, psychological, and emotional health of individuals. The practice will continue to flourish for a long time to come.

My goal with this book is to help you assess your house now and learn about the options available with universal design, so that you can make informed decisions about creating an attractive, comfortable, eco-friendly, and safe home for the next chapter of your life. After you read this book, you may decide to renovate your kitchen or bedroom, change the shower in the bathroom, or update your living room furniture. Or you may realize you need to move to another house that better meets your future needs.

Working with this book, you'll:

1. Learn about basic universal design features that are helpful for everyone, regardless of age or ability.

2. Be able to walk through each room of the house, and even through outdoor spaces, and see which products and construction ideas can be individualized for specific physical limitations and health conditions common among older adults.

3. Learn what you can do today, easily and inexpensively, to improve the livability of your home. Scattered throughout the book are Quick Fixes that give you specific information to help you make simple changes, especially if remodeling is not an option.

4. Be able to communicate more knowledgeably about universal design features when you talk with contractors, which will help ensure that you get the results you desire.

5. Learn about green practices that complement universal design; the Easy to Go Green sections highlight those practices.

6. Focus on the importance of your own habits and lifestyle preferences that, when incorporated into a universally designed home, contribute to beautiful and safe living. Longevity Essentials will give you information on everything from exercising at home to how social networks improve your physical well-being. In addition, you'll find tips in It's Wise to Be Safe that will help you prevent accidents and other mishaps.

7. Learn how to take a good look at your community and decide whether or not it's the type of environment that stands ready to provide the amenities and services you'll require as you age. And if you decide to move into a new 50+ community, you'll be armed with the essential questions you'll need to ask to see if you can truly "age in place" there.

So read on and discover all of the many exciting, effective ways that universal design can promote wellness at home for a longer and more fulfilling life.

Planning for an accessible home is a smart choice because we're living longer. This first-floor bathroom, for example, has a walk-in shower with a partial glass wall that allows natural light to flood the room. The window provides fresh air and ventilation, which helps to reduce indoor pollutants.

CHAPTER 1

Forward Thinking

LIFE IS FULL OF SURPRISES and never more so than in the second half. Although adults over age 50 are staying healthier and more active than previous generations, *change happens*. To a large extent, how well we adapt to change depends on our attitude, our lifestyle, our community re-sources—*and our home's design*. The good news is that universal design can greatly increase our ability to live for many years in the comfort of our own home.

In this chapter I will explain four key prin-ciples of universal design and introduce you to the myriad ways you can apply them to your situation. Ideally you'll be able to make changes to your existing home that fit your budget and address your specific needs. Whether you simply update furnish-ings or add a first-floor master bedroom, you'll discover that universal design fea-tures can help you live a more confident and active lifestyle.

As we face the new realities of these finan-cially challenging times, modifying our current home to suit our changing needs can be a more affordable option than an assisted-living residence or other form of institutional care. And, if eventually you need to move, these modifications may have increased the value of your home.

The Origins of Universal Design

Universal design was developed by Ron Mace, the visionary architect who founded the Center for Universal Design at North Carolina State University in Raleigh. Mace, who used a wheelchair ever since he contracted polio as a child, had two particularly important insights. First, the "average," normal, completely healthy person who an architect has in mind when designing the typical house doesn't exist, for all practical purposes. For example, it isn't likely that a counter height appropriate for a man who is 6 foot (1.8 m) tall will be equally functional for a woman who is 6 or 7 inches (15 or 18 cm) shorter. Plus, as Mace observed in a 1998 speech, "We all become disabled as we age and lose ability, whether we want to admit it or not." The other thing Mace noticed is that features designed to make life easier for persons with disabilities made life easier for everyone. For instance, those sloped curbs designed for wheelchair users also benefit bicyclists and parents pushing strollers.

Universal design promotes safe, accessible living. A home with a no-step entryway, wide doorways, and plenty of first-floor living space provides a user-friendly environment for a lifetime.

Universal Design = Benefits for Everyone

Put simply, universal design is, well, *universal*. One of its primary goals is to create a house—the structure, everything that fills it, and the outdoor spaces that surround it—that is usable by everyone right now: boomers with knee replacements, young families with baby carriages, elderly parents, teenagers on crutches after a snowboarding accident, or anyone who uses a walker, scooter, or wheelchair.

Although universal design is better for everyone, it's especially beneficial as our physical and health conditions change with age, and it becomes more difficult to bend, walk, grasp, and see well. Typical homes and products can frustrate even the most patient among us. But universal design's user-friendly features make it easier for those with common age-related conditions to function at their maximum capability.

A universal design home is like a best friend who's there for you both in good times and when the going gets rough. If and when unexpected events happen—you're ready! With a bit of planning, you'll be able to relax, knowing that if a crisis occurs, you or a loved one can continue living in your own home to the *maximum* extent possible.

A first-floor master bedroom with access to an outside patio makes for easy and gracious living.

Increased Vitality

According to AARP, the overwhelming majority of individuals over the age of 45—a full 89 percent of Americans—want to remain in their current residence and never move. If you are like most older adults who currently require or anticipate needing a certain amount of help caring for yourself, you'd prefer to receive services in your own home instead of depending on institutional care. This trend is referred to as "aging in place."

We also know that there won't be enough nursing homes or assisted-living residences for those considering these alternative housing arrangements. That's due to the sheer numbers of the 50+ crowd. For the first time in history, U.S. citizens over 50 outnumber those under 25. One-third of the nation's population—a staggering 75 million people—are baby boomers between ages 44 and 64. Not only are more of us living longer, but we're also living to very advanced ages. The U.S. Census Bureau projects that one out of nine boomers will live well into their 90s, and that one in 26 will live to be 100 years old. These new demographic realities will reverberate dramatically in society over the next several decades on many different levels.

The Challenge

Most of us believe that illness and disability happen only to others. But sooner or later we have to face the fact that we all have to cope with changing physical capacities and health problems as we age. And we're bound to discover that it's never easy to make clear-headed decisions in the midst of a health crisis when our world is turned upside down, suddenly fraught with obstacles and unpleasant challenges.

Livable homes and communities offer easy access to the outdoors, so vital to our health and happiness.

It turns out that one of the main obstacles to continuing to live at home is the house itself. Quite often, it's the simple everyday tasks, like getting into the bathroom or up and down the stairs that become the greatest barriers to independent living. Typical houses are designed to accommodate users who are young and healthy. The old way of design, established in the early 1900s for the "average" person who lived only until their mid-40s, is out of date in today's world, where more than half of us are over 50 and one in five has a disability.

So how, specifically, can universal design help us live independently in our own homes? Although there are seven recognized principles in universal design, I have shortened and consolidated them into four key principles that are most relevant as you consider making changes to your home.

Four Key Design Principles

At first glance, universal design homes look like regular homes. But take a closer look and you'll notice that the layout of the house, the furnishings, flooring, bathroom fixtures, kitchen appliances, door handles, lighting, and many household "gadgets" are designed with four key principles in mind. Those design principles enable you or anyone else to live comfortably, effortlessly, and safely in the same structure for a lifetime. And as you'll see, although the principles overlap to a degree, each one is essential, and they work together beautifully.

1. Ease of Use

The goal of universal design is to make life easier. A vegetable peeler with a cushioned handle, crank-style windows that someone of average strength can open, a stove with large controls in easy-to-see colors—everything in a universal design home is intended to require a minimum amount of physical and mental effort. Materials are chosen for ease of maintenance, such as surfaces that you don't have to paint every few years and a yard that doesn't require weekly mowing.

2. Getting Around

It's possible that at some point you may not be able to climb stairs, or you may need to use a walker, wheelchair, or scooter. Designing to accommodate the needs of people who use these mobility aids entails certain specific features. These include no-step entrances; wide doorways; adequate turning radius within a space, especially in smaller rooms such as bathrooms; and open floor space throughout the home. Ideally, interior door openings should have a minimum of 34 to 36 inches (86 to 91 cm) of clear open space. This width is not only graceful, elegant, and aesthetically pleasing, but it also makes carrying in large packages and moving furniture easier. Universal design halls are at least 42 inches (107 cm) wide, instead of the standard 36 inches (91 cm), to allow for greater ease of movement.

Every room should include a 5-foot (1.5 m) turning radius—in other words, a cleared area 5 feet in

Battery-operated can openers are user-friendly for the entire family because they require little effort to operate.

A rolling knife is easier to use than a standard knife. It puts less pressure on the joints, which allows you to prepare food in comfort.

Open, spacious rooms can be stylish and allow everyone to move through and between areas with ease and grace.

This functional and aesthetically pleasing ramp blends in with the home design and offers an accessible user-friendly entrance for everyone.

diameter that allows you to turn a wheelchair or walker around completely. But an open layout doesn't benefit just people using mobility aids. Are you constantly bumping up against your partner or spouse as you cook? Create a roomy kitchen and you'll both be happier.

The simplest, most straightforward example of a no-step entrance is a nicely landscaped, gradually sloping entranceway. Other options include permanent or temporary ramps, attractively woven into the landscape with shrubs and flower boxes, or a porch lift than can comfortably accommodate standing or seated users.

3. Flexibility

Universal design's approach recognizes that at any given point in time, a house is likely to have many users, each of whom has different abilities and needs. In addition, those abilities and needs change over time. So a universal design house includes

adaptable interior features to allow each user a customized fit—both now and in the future. There's really no reason other than tradition that your home must be designed with permanently fixed interior features. For example, motorized height-adjustable sinks make grooming and doing the dishes equally convenient and comfortable for a 6-foot (1.8 m) man, a 5-foot-5-inch (1.6 m) woman, or a household member in a wheelchair. And the more designers build adaptability into the original design,

the more economical universal design is. For instance, if home builders made a practice of stacking one closet above the other on different floors, those closets could easily be converted into an elevator shaft at less expense than if a new one had to be built.

4. Safe, Healthy Living

The universal home includes design features that can reduce the risk of accidents, including falls, the major cause of injury among older adults. Did you know that one in three persons over age 65 falls each year, and that every 18 seconds an older adult is treated in an emergency room as the result of a fall? That's why adequate lighting and non-slip flooring are essential features of a universal home. Eliminating steps and stairs wherever practical is important, too, as is making sure that the remaining stairs are as safe as possible. To prevent household fires, homeowners should make sure that all electrical wiring is up to date and can make use of new smart technologies that help prevent fires and quickly extinguish them if they should break out.

An open kitchen with a place to eat is ideal for casual dining and family gatherings. The generous floor plan makes it easy to move around, and the half wall allows light to flow through interior spaces.

In addition to making the home a safer place to live, designing your home the universal way is a great route to go green. You can choose eco-friendly flooring, fabrics made from natural or recycled fibers, and paint and wallpaper with low VOC (volatile organic compounds) ratings, which are better for the environment *and* for you.

The universal home is designed for both safety and comfort. For example, an anti-slip cushioned floor mat helps reduce leg and back strain while it prevents slipping in wet areas. Choose a mat with a beveled edge to reduce any chance of tripping over it.

Smart Design Can = Beautiful Living

Universal design options are stylish as well as functional, so you can remodel and refurnish your home without the risk of turning it into an institutional-looking residence. In fact, a golden rule in this approach to interior features, furnishings, and everyday products is to design with attractiveness in mind. No one wants "handicapped" design that's ugly and stigmatizing. Having a health condition or impairment certainly doesn't mean you lose interest in beauty and comfort! And, of course, a key element of any home design is the individuality it reflects. Your home should embody your needs, your preferences, and even your eccentricities.

There are so many good reasons to choose universal design features for your home. To summarize the benefits, universal design offers:

1. An accessible, safe, and welcoming environment, both outside and inside your home, for you and everyone else, regardless of their ability.

2. An insurance policy for your future that allows you to maintain a healthy lifestyle as your needs change.

3. A sound financial investment. Incorporating universal design into remodeling projects often adds little or no cost to renovations. What's more, your home's value probably will increase due to the rapidly growing demand for housing that accommodates needs throughout a lifespan. And, it's becoming clear that staying in an existing house is likely to be far less expensive than institutional care.

This spacious, open floor plan offers a choice of seating for different needs, well-illuminated rooms, and wide entryways for safe passage.

CHAPTER 2

Planning for a Lifetime

UNIVERSAL DESIGN is a smart choice for today's new longevity. Its greatest feature is its capacity to accommodate people's changing needs throughout their lifetime. No wonder universal design is fast becoming the new "must have" design.

Living well in the second half of your life requires smart planning that includes a comfortable, user-friendly home that serves you well if you remain healthy and active. But should anything happen, it will also enhance your ability to function independently.

If you're between ages 50 and 90, my advice is simple: it's time for you to look at your residence to determine how well it suits your current lifestyle and what would be involved in adapting it to meet your future needs.

Taking Stock

In this chapter, I'll show you how to take a personal inventory of your needs. I'll also explain how to conduct a "walk-through" and apply universal design principles to every room in your home, so you can plan and make the changes necessary to turn your house into a lifetime home. This type of planning requires a straightforward appraisal of your own personal life situation, or that of an older parent—both now and in the future.

Personal Inventory of Needs

In thinking through the questions that follow, be honest. Conducting a personal inventory will save you time, money, and aggravation in the long run. Planning now for your future can bring you greater peace and comfort as you age. It's a bit like buying life insurance or writing your will. No one wants to think about disability or end-of-life issues, but you do it for the benefit of everyone involved: your children, your spouse, *and* yourself.

Your personal inventory will help you sort out which home features you'll need to live a safer, healthier lifestyle and to retain your independence. Moreover, the ease of use that's an essential part of the universal home benefits anyone who might be a caregiver in the future. Knowing that you're prepared will give you peace of mind.

So let's begin the planning stage!

Carving out a corner for an attractive home office is easier than you think when you use spacing-saving sliding doors. Perhaps you'll start a small business and manage it in a space just like this one.

Age

What is your age? What is the likelihood that you'll be in your home for the next decade or more?

Gender

If you're a woman and you're either married or have an aging parent, statistics say there's a good chance you'll be a caregiver at some point in your life. The right home setup can eliminate the struggles often associated with caregiving and provide you—and the person you're caring for—more opportunities for continued enjoyment of life. Preparing your home to take care of a loved one and helping him or her to live with ease and dignity is one of the greatest gifts you can offer.

Another fact to consider: statistics tell us that 79 percent of all adults over 65 who live alone are women. If your objective is to remain in your home—either on your own, with friends, or with another family member—plan now for the modifications that will enable you to do so. Knowing that you can stay in your home for as long as you wish and be as independent as possible can offer comfort during difficult times of change.

Physical Condition

Take stock of your physical condition at the moment. Are you already coping with any age-related changes, such as vision or hearing loss or difficulties with mobility? Even if you're not experiencing any significant problems in these areas, you need to be realistic and imagine how comfortable and safe your home will be in 10, 20, 30, or more years.

Keep in mind that, even if you don't own your home or apartment, you have the right to change your living space to enhance your ability

A universally designed home enhances your ability to maintain social connections vital to healthy longevity by allowing all of your friends and loved ones to visit, regardless of their abilities.

to function. (See chapter 10, From Plan to Reality, on page 196 for a more in-depth discussion of the Fair Housing Act.)

Visitors

Universal design's inclusionary philosophy recognizes the importance of community to our overall well-being and enjoyment of life. Therefore, it's important to look at who else uses your home. Do you have friends who frequently come over to cook together and share a meal? Do other family members think of your home as a central gathering place for holidays and celebratory events? If so, does your home really accommodate the needs of everyone, young and old, who use it? If a best friend could no longer climb stairs, would she be able to enter your home and use a bathroom if needed? A few design changes could make access possible for all your visitors.

Your Community

As we age, the saying "no one is an island" takes on greater significance. A "livable community" promotes quality of life by providing amenities and services essential for healthy aging. Public transportation, wide sidewalks with curb cuts, accessible shopping, and medical services within reach are all part of what defines a community as "livable." Does your community offer these kinds of services? What if you or a neighbor needed help with grocery shopping and meal preparation?

Your Budget

A limited budget doesn't have to prevent you from making effective changes to your home; neither does an unlimited budget guarantee a perfect redesign. The key is to understand your personal needs and prioritize them. A low-cost change that meets a high-priority need may give you the biggest bang for your buck. For example, although light levels can be challenging for anyone, they're particularly unsafe if you have a visual impairment. You could greatly enhance your safety and the usability of your home by simply purchasing some new energy-efficient lamps. As we go through each chapter, I'll be giving suggestions on both small- and large-scale changes you can make.

As you reconsider the cost of renovations or new furnishings, it's important to compare those immediate expenses to the cost of alternative living arrangements if you were to move out of your home. Keep in mind, too, that investing in features such as a first-floor master bedroom and bath will increase the value of your home, should you decide to sell it.

Evaluating What You Have

It's time for your home walk-through. Until you assess what you already have, you won't know where to begin to achieve your goal of making your home suitable for your entire life. This checklist is full of universal design features that can make your home more user-friendly for you, your family, and anyone else, regardless of age or ability.

This universal kitchen has a center island that offers convenient sit-down dining or buffet style meals for larger gatherings.

When assessing your stairs, think of all the people who might use them. Heavily patterned carpeting, as pictured here, can be unsafe as it often distorts visual perception. When choosing stair carpeting, look for a plain or a lightly patterned design, with a low pile.

The Walk-Through

Let's begin with the exterior of your home and then work our way inside. Give an honest answer to everything on the list and write down any questions or issues that come up.

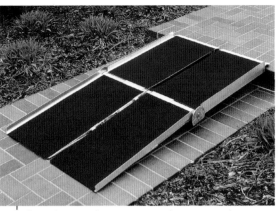

If you have only one or two short steps, you may be able to create an accessible entrance with a portable ramp. Some can even be folded so you can carry them easily.

Outside Checklist

This sloped walkway leads to an accessible entrance through the home's backyard.

Accessibility	Yes	No
Level or gently sloping walkway to entrance	☐	☐
Ramp to front door or garage	☐	☐
No-step entrance to house through garage or back of house	☐	☐
No or low threshold at main doors into house	☐	☐
Lever-style door handles	☐	☐
Doorways are 36 inches (91.5 cm) wide or have swing-clear hinges to improve clearance for mobility devices	☐	☐

Safer Stairs	Yes	No
Stairs in good repair	☐	☐
Handrails on both sides of stairs	☐	☐
Covered entryway	☐	☐
Easy-open deadbolt locks on doors	☐	☐

Safety	Yes	No
Easy-to-use peephole or side shatterproof glass panels	☐	☐
Even, smooth walkways without cracks	☐	☐
Good lighting along walkways and at entryway	☐	☐
Easily visible home address, including at nighttime	☐	☐

Vision-Friendly	Yes	No
Good lighting from garage or street to front door	☐	☐
Illuminated doorbell	☐	☐
Edges of steps are highlighted	☐	☐

Outside Checklist

Comfort & Convenience	Yes	No
Doorbell wired throughout the house, or wireless doorbell and chimes added to commonly used rooms	☐	☐
Low-maintenance exterior materials	☐	☐
Outdoor space with comfortable seating and sun protection	☐	☐
Accessible gardening	☐	☐

Go Green	Yes	No
Retractable awnings to reduce interior heat gain in summer	☐	☐
Landscaping that blocks summer sun and allows winter light	☐	☐
Low-voltage, solar, or LED lighting	☐	☐
Rainwater tank for gardening/lawn maintenance	☐	☐
Eco-friendly deck, patio, and flooring materials	☐	☐

Notes

General Interior Features Checklist

Interior Routes, Layouts & Doors	Yes	No
Unimpeded (furniture-free) routes from room to room and within rooms	☐	☐
No thresholds or low, beveled thresholds	☐	☐
Hallways 42 inches (107 cm) wide	☐	☐
Doors 36 inches (91.5 cm) wide or swing-clear hinges	☐	☐
Turning radius of 5 feet (1.5 m) in all rooms	☐	☐

Windows	Yes	No
Easy to open	☐	☐

This welcoming entryway has a range of user-friendly features, including a wide doorway with a side panel window that lets you see who's outside; an attractive, easy-to-use lever door handle; and wooden flooring with a matte finish.

If your stairway has only one handrail, consider installing another to make climbing the stairs safer and easier for everyone, especially for those with one side stronger than the other.

Flooring

	Yes	No
Nonslip flooring or low-pile, low-maintenance carpet	☐	☐
Area rugs with anti-slip pads or taped to floor with double-sided tape	☐	☐
Floors have matte, not polished, finish	☐	☐

Stair Safety

	Yes	No
Handrails securely installed on both sides, 33–36 inches (84–91.5 cm) from the stair, 1½ inches (4 cm) from the wall, and 1½ inches (4 cm) in diameter	☐	☐
Handrails extend 12 inches (30.5 cm) beyond the last step on the wall side when possible	☐	☐
Edges of steps highlighted	☐	☐
Wall color contrasts with handrails	☐	☐
Open risers closed off	☐	☐
Light switch installed at both top and bottom of stairs	☐	☐

Go Green

	Yes	No
Energy-efficient windows	☐	☐
Eco-friendly doors, flooring, and finishes	☐	☐

This handsome bathroom has plenty of storage space and an adjacent walk-in closet/dressing area. The sleek pocket door has a translucent glass front, allowing light to pass through, and there is no closet threshold to trip over.

Notes

Lighting & Electric Checklist

Accessibility	Yes	No
Light switches installed 44–48 inches (112–122 cm) above floor	☐	☐
Electrical outlets, cable, telephone, and modem jacks installed 18–42 inches (46–107 cm) above floor	☐	☐
Circuit breakers located on main floor	☐	☐

Safety	Yes	No
Three-way switches on all stair lighting	☐	☐
Wall electrical outlets in use instead of extension cords across floor	☐	☐
Even lighting throughout home, including hallways and stairs	☐	☐
Ample electrical circuits to prevent blown fuses and accommodate future home technologies	☐	☐
Waterproof light in shower area	☐	☐
Night-lights in hallways, bedrooms, bathrooms, and other rooms traversed at night	☐	☐

This kitchen has many well-designed universal features. Good lighting, including the bright range-hood downlights, illuminates the work surfaces for safer cooking. A lower countertop helps those who need to sit while preparing food. An easy-to-maintain, slip-resistant floor prevents accidents. The microwave is safely positioned on the countertop; people burn themselves when removing hot food from an overhead microwave.

Vision-Friendly	Yes	No
Automatic closet lighting or battery-operated LED lights for touch turn-on and turn-off	☐	☐
Under-counter lighting in kitchen	☐	☐
Color of light switch contrasts with wall color	☐	☐
Bright, glare-free light available for each specific activity area	☐	☐
Appliance controls with large, color-contrasted words/numbers	☐	☐

Comfort & Convenience	Yes	No
Illuminated, rocker-style light switch or sensor light installed at entrance to every room	☐	☐
Polyester film, sheer curtains, shades, or blinds on windows for glare reduction	☐	☐
Dimmer switches for built-in, flexible light levels	☐	☐
Handheld remote for lighting	☐	☐

Kitchen Checklist

Go Green
	Yes	No
Heating and cooling for different parts of the house on separate thermostats	☐	☐
Large windows and skylights provide natural light	☐	☐
Energy-saving thermostat and other controls	☐	☐
Energy-efficient lighting (fluorescent and LED) throughout home	☐	☐
Eco-friendly window treatments	☐	☐
Solar panels and other sources of alternative energy	☐	☐

Notes

Accessibility
	Yes	No
Elevated dishwasher at back-friendly height, about 9 inches (23 cm) from the floor (or at a comfortable and convenient height)	☐	☐
Wall-mounted oven with side opening and pull-out ledge underneath	☐	☐
A 30 x 48-inch (76 x 122 cm) area of clear floor space in front of all appliances	☐	☐
Varied-height countertops for standing and sitting	☐	☐

Safety
	Yes	No
Nonslip, matte-finish, low-maintenance flooring	☐	☐
Automatic shut-off timers on cooking appliances	☐	☐
Automatic fire extinguishers in range hood	☐	☐
Microwave installed on or below countertop	☐	☐
Stove controls located on front or side	☐	☐
Fire extinguishers accessible and in working order (and you know how to use them!)	☐	☐
Long sink sprayer hose to fill pots at stovetop	☐	☐
Anti-scald control at sink	☐	☐

Vision-Friendly
	Yes	No
Countertop with matte surface to reduce glare	☐	☐
Countertop color contrasts with floor	☐	☐

Ease of Use
	Yes	No
Faucet with two lever-style handles or a single lever	☐	☐
C style handles on doors and cabinets	☐	☐
Ergonomic kitchen tools with large, cushioned handles	☐	☐

Universal design promotes comfort and convenience. In the kitchen, this translates into a raised dishwasher to reduce excessive bending and minimize back strain.

Kitchen Checklist

Comfort & Convenience	Yes	No
Comfortable chair or stool for seating	☐	☐
Cushioned, nonslip mat for standing by sink and in food-prep areas	☐	☐
"Quiet" model appliances	☐	☐
Pot-filler faucet at stovetop	☐	☐
"Passing" window from kitchen to living/dining area	☐	☐

Go Green	Yes	No
Eco-friendly countertops, flooring, and cabinetry	☐	☐
Energy-efficient appliances	☐	☐
Recycling containers	☐	☐
Composting	☐	☐
Range hood to improve indoor air quality	☐	☐

Notes

This cheerful kitchen has abundant natural and interior lighting. There's a comfortable place to plan meals, grab a snack, or prepare food. A window-seat garden merges indoor and outdoor living, and is a great place to grow plants and herbs.

Living & Dining Room Checklist

Accessibility	Yes	No
Seating is easy to get in and out of	☐	☐
Turning radius of 5 feet (1.5 m)	☐	☐

Safety	Yes	No
Nonslip flooring or low-pile, low-maintenance carpet	☐	☐
Area rugs with anti-slip pads or taped to floor with double-sided tape	☐	☐
Matte-finish, not polished, flooring	☐	☐
Wall electrical outlets in use instead of extension cords across floor	☐	☐

Vision-Friendly	Yes	No
Abundant lighting for "walking around" and completing tasks	☐	☐
Window treatments filter sunlight and reduce glare	☐	☐
Table surfaces are matte finish, not polished	☐	☐
Color of chairs and sofa contrasts with floor	☐	☐
Large TV	☐	☐
Easy-to-read, large-font TV remote controls	☐	☐

Comfort & Convenience	Yes	No
Lighting on dimmer switches	☐	☐
Handheld lighting controls	☐	☐

Large windows fill this attractive dining room with natural light. A matte finish on the wood flooring offers safe footing.

Go Green	Yes	No
Reused (second-hand) furniture	☐	☐
Natural fiber for upholstery, flooring, and window treatments	☐	☐

Notes

Need to brighten a dim room? One quick fix: place an eco-friendly torchiere lamp (with a fluorescent bulb) in a corner to boost overall lighting. Natural woven window shades filter harsh sunlight.

Bathroom Checklist

Accessibility	Yes	No
Walk-in/wheel-in capacity	☐	☐
No threshold or low, beveled threshold	☐	☐
Large, walk-in/wheel-in shower, or transfer bench for use with bathtub and hand-held showerhead	☐	☐
Bathtub with side ledge for easy entering	☐	☐
Walk-in bathtub with door	☐	☐
Grab bars in bathing area attached securely to the wall	☐	☐
Toilet seat height at 17–18 inches (43–46 cm)	☐	☐
Securely attached grab bars near toilet	☐	☐
Sink usable in seated position, if necessary	☐	☐
Medicine cabinet installed on a side wall for an easier reach	☐	☐

Safety	Yes	No
Anti-scald protection in shower, bathtub, and sink	☐	☐
Privacy lock for door (can be opened from outside the bathroom in case of emergency)	☐	☐
Textured, slip-resistant flooring inside shower and bathtub	☐	☐
Slip-resistant flooring	☐	☐
Anti-skid backing on floor mats	☐	☐
Telephone or other communication available	☐	☐

Multiple luxurious sprays offer an invigorating spa-like shower experience that can be therapeutic and relaxing.

This ergonomic handheld shower provides an invigorating, easily controlled spray. It is a stylish option in the universal bathing area for showering while seated.

A shower entrance without a threshold is an ideal feature in a universal design bathroom. A sloping drain keeps the water in the shower, and the dark border provides an important visual contrast.

Vision-Friendly	Yes	No
Magnifying mirror for easier grooming	☐	☐
Good lighting	☐	☐
Wall sconces (with shades) on each side of mirror above sink, even overhead light	☐	☐
Illuminated light switches	☐	☐
Color of grab bars contrasts with wall color	☐	☐
Color of toilet seat contrasts with floor	☐	☐
Nighttime lighting	☐	☐

Ease of Use	Yes	No
Lever-style faucets and door handles	☐	☐
Ergonomic, large, cushioned, handheld showerhead	☐	☐

Comfort & Convenience	Yes	No
Ceiling heat lamp	☐	☐
Quiet exhaust fan	☐	☐

Go Green	Yes	No
Low-flow toilet	☐	☐
Low-flow showerhead	☐	☐
Radiant flooring	☐	☐
Rainwater tank for showering/bathing needs	☐	☐

Notes

This clever toilet space has a partial wall on a hinge that can be swung out of the way to make room for a walker, a wheelchair, or a caregiver.

As universal design has no particular style, you can choose any look to express your personality. For example, this vanity area has modern, uncluttered lines but can be used by someone who needs to be seated while at the sink.

IT'S WISE TO BE SAFE

Lower Water Temperature
Hot water set at 120°F (49°C) to prevent scalding can be a problem for individuals undergoing chemotherapy or with compromised health. These lower temperatures can increase their risk for Legionnaires Disease. The World Health Organization recommends setting your hot water heater temperature at 140°F (60°C) and installing anti-scalding devices to deliver water at safer, lower temperatures.

Bedroom Checklist

Accessibility | Yes | No
First-floor-accessible bedroom (including Murphy bed or sleep sofa, if needed) ☐ ☐

No threshold or low, beveled threshold ☐ ☐

Adequate room for mobility aids, with 3 feet (91.5 cm) of clear space on two sides of the bed and 5 feet (1.5 m) of clear space on the third side ☐ ☐

Bed surface at safe height (when seated on edge of bed, your knees should be level with your hips while your feet remain flat on the floor) ☐ ☐

Accessibility | Yes | No
Adjustable closet rods and shelving ☐ ☐

Safety | Yes | No
Nonslip flooring or low-pile, low-maintenance carpet ☐ ☐

Area rugs with anti-slip pads or taped to floor with double-sided tape ☐ ☐

Vision-Friendly | Yes | No
Bedside light within easy reach ☐ ☐

Telephone with large illuminated numbers for nighttime emergency use ☐ ☐

Vision-Friendly | Yes | No
Nighttime illumination for walking path from bedroom to bathroom ☐ ☐

Color-contrasting or illuminated light switch at entrance ☐ ☐

Bedding and seating color contrasts with floor ☐ ☐

Ease of Use | Yes | No
Large handles on dressers and side tables (not round knobs) ☐ ☐

Lever-style door handles ☐ ☐

While not a permanent option, a Murphy bed could allow you, a loved one, or a guest to sleep on the ground floor.

Environmental Controls	Yes	No
Bedside environmental controls (for example: lighting, window treatment, security, remote video door-answering system)	☐	☐

Comfort & Convenience	Yes	No
Supportive, comfortable mattress	☐	☐

Go Green	Yes	No
Natural fiber for bedding, flooring, and window treatments	☐	☐
Plants and air purifier for better air quality	☐	☐

Notes

How to Use This Checklist

Congratulations! You've finished the walk-through! If you're like most people, you've identified several things you'd like to improve to make your home more comfortable and accessible. The good news is that there are many no- and low-cost changes you can make to the exterior and interior of your home, and I'll be discussing them as we proceed through the book, room by room. You'll discover various ways to make improvements that meet your needs, your lifestyle, and your budget. When you come across an idea that appeals to you, come back to this checklist and jot down the solutions that work for you.

Top 12 Universal Design Features

Over the years, people have asked me to list the universal design features that I think are essential. I've boiled that list down to an even dozen. As you'll see, designing for a lifetime is not about spending a lot of money. It's about thinking through the most important changes you can make to enjoy a healthy, long, and fulfilling life. My list addresses the three main barriers to aging in place: difficulty getting in and out of the home, difficulty getting around the home, and an inaccessible bathroom.

1. A no-step entry to your home

2. Wider doorways and hallways

3. Walk-in, no-threshold shower

4. A bedroom and bathroom on the first floor

5. Reachable, rocker-style light switches*

6. Lever-style door handles and faucets

7. Kitchen appliances with automatic shut-off features

8. Non-slip flooring, especially in the kitchen and bathroom**

9. Abundant and even lighting

10. Grab bars in bathing areas

11. Comfortable furniture and furnishings

12. Telephones and doorbells with low-frequency tones

*A rocker switch requires less strength and dexterity than the standard toggle switch. To turn the light on or off, you just push in on the top or bottom of the switch; it's silent, simple, and can be illuminated for easy finding in the dark.

**Whenever possible, remove areas rugs. Even if you use non-slip pads and tape the rugs to the floor, you may still find area rugs present a tripping hazard.

This dining area uses both natural light and electric light, including a hanging pendant lamp, to brighten the space. A larger area carpet would make this dining area even more accessible, as no chair legs or wheels (or paws) would rest off the carpet.

Gallery

For the first time in the history of interior-design show houses, gorgeous and stylish universal rooms were on display at the 2006 Livable Lifetime Show House in Fayetteville, Georgia. More than 17 designers collaborated, weaving accessibility features seamlessly into the home designs with ease, style, and grace—the true spirit of universal design. Pictured here is a den designed by Carol Axford of CDA Design Group that is fashionable and light-filled, functional and flexible. Among other universal design elements, it features easy-to-open C handles on the file drawers, low-pile carpet, and rounded corners on the furniture.

CHAPTER 3

The Big Picture

Your home is your refuge, or at least it should be. With a little planning, you can dramatically increase your ability to live there independently. In this chapter, we'll be looking at the big picture—ways that you can incorporate universal design features throughout your house so that living there is easier and more comfortable. From lighting and heating to accessibility and safety, we'll look at products and technologies that simplify life and conserve energy.

We'll also explore how specific interior features, from the latest home elevator systems to the safest flooring choices, can make your home more accessible while keeping you safe. Finally, we'll review a range of new smart technologies that you'll appreciate in the second half of your life.

easy to go green
What Is Energy Star?

Items marked "Energy Star" are appliances and fixtures designed to use less energy, save you money, and reduce the amount of pollution that contributes to global warming. To earn the Energy Star label, products must meet the guidelines set by the U.S. Environmental Protection Agency and the Department of Energy (DOE). As Energy Star does not restrict styles, you can still choose the look you're after, whether it's old-world traditional or sleek and modern. More than 40 types of products have earned Energy Star labels, including lighting, kitchen appliances, heating and air conditioning equipment, and even entire new homes.

LEARN MORE AT
energystar.gov

Buyer Beware!

In 2009, the Energy Star program came under close scrutiny by *Consumer Reports*, whose testing of refrigerators revealed lower energy ratings than those given by Energy Star. *Consumer Reports* cites two main reasons for the discrepancy:

1. The *manufacturer*—not DOE—tests the products for energy efficiency and submits the results to DOE, which relies solely on the manufacturer's claims; and

2. A number of DOE's mandated tests are out of date.

Now that reducing energy consumption is on everyone's radar, including DOE's and consumers', look for more efficient government controls in the near future. Do your homework before buying any appliance. *Consumer Reports* is a good resource for this.

Lighting

Lighting is a key universal design element that promotes healthy longevity, helping you see and function better. Bright, well-lit rooms can improve your ability to perform tasks, enhance your mood, and keep you from falling. Lighting is a valuable tool for creating a pleasing décor; it can, for instance, make a small room seem larger.

Free-flowing spaces make it easy to navigate and allow light to pass through. Recessed ceiling lights provide ample illumination. Warm-colored walls, paired with a light floor finish, help keep the space open and airy.

Lighting Strategies

Everyone enjoys a beautiful, well-lit room, especially older adults. Did you know we need a lot more light—some specialists say three times more—to see as well in our 50s as we did when we were 20?

Since quality is just as important as quantity, in the universal home we use glare-free lighting that's warm and comforting to the eyes. When it comes to creating glare, the main culprits are brilliant daylight, glossy surfaces, and bare bulbs. Here are a few things you can do to enhance your visual comfort:

• Use adjustable blinds or sheer curtains to soften and filter bright, incoming daylight.

• Refinish glossy surfaces (like highly polished wood floors and walls with high-gloss paint) with a matte finish, as the reflected light from a shiny finish can be harsh to the eye, especially if you have low vision.

• Cover all exposed bulbs with lampshades, since glare from bare bulbs can cause headaches and decrease vision.

Also, we can be temporarily blinded when moving from bright to low light levels. For example, when entering a dark foyer on a bright sunny day, it takes longer for our eyes to adjust. That's why a universal lighting scheme includes adjustable light levels throughout the house. Three-way bulbs or dimmer switches are a much-welcomed feature, allowing people to customize the lighting to their unique needs.

Light Up the Night!

You can create soft lighting schemes that result in a warm and welcoming atmosphere simply by using three-way bulbs and dimmer switches. Another option is to install a wall

These eco-friendly, handwoven shades allow glare-free light to filter into the room while keeping the interior heat from building up.

valance that fills a room with soft, indirect lighting.

Night lighting also plays an important role in keeping you safe. For example, illuminated rocker light switches instead of the toggle variety in the entryway of each room or hall help prevent you and your guests from fumbling for the light switch in the dark. In addition, automatic LED night-lights in the bedroom, bathroom, and hall enhance nighttime safety, illuminating obstacles like the sleeping cat sprawled in the doorway. LED night-lights are available in soft, luminous colors and are eco-friendly, costing only pennies a year to operate. And this highlights yet another reason why dimmer switches are such a good idea: you can leave table lamps or ceiling lights on low all through the night so you never have to wander around in the dark.

Night-lights promote safety for anyone walking after dark, especially in areas where the floor level changes. LED night-lights are an excellent choice as they provide good illumination, are eco-friendly, and cost little.

Choosing a Light Fixture

You can choose from many different kinds of light fixtures, depending on whether you need general "walking around" light or close-up task lighting.

For general lighting in a room, choose:

• Tall table lamps with light-colored shades and wide-bottom shade openings. They'll light a larger area than smaller lamps, thus enhancing the room's overall lighting; the shade's bottom should be level with your eyes when you're seated. If you can see the bulb, replace the shade with one that fits better.

• Regular floor lamps or "torchieres" (floor lamps that direct light toward the ceiling) with fluorescent bulbs.

Placing a torchiere in a corner is a particularly good choice if you want to give your room a real boost in lighting.

• Three-way bulbs to offer flexibility in light levels.

• Indirect lighting, including valances, to fill in shadows and create a soft, glare-free space.

If you're thinking about recessed or track lighting, consider its placement carefully to avoid disorienting scallops of light that are sometimes produced by this type of lighting.

For close-up task lighting aimed directly on an object, such as a book or computer keyboard, invest in a quality lamp with:

• A flexible neck that allows you to pull the light down close to your task.

• An internal reflector (such as a double shade) to reduce the heat.

Be wary of inexpensive lamps: you might well find that it's harder to position such a light exactly where you need it. And usually the lower quality lamps produce more glare, because they have heat-venting slots on the shade, allowing harsh light to shine through.

Choosing a Lightbulb

New technologies have created a variety of high-quality bulbs, some more efficient than others. As there's no one light bulb that's best for everyone or for every activity, test various bulbs until you find what works for you. You may find that full-spectrum bulbs are good for close-up tasks where color rendition is important, while compact fluorescent lightbulbs (CFLs) are ideal for general lighting.

Finding the right bulb, however, can be confusing due to the enormous variety on the market today—and sometimes the information you need to choose wisely can be highly technical. Below is a brief description of the various lightbulbs along with tips on what to look for when purchasing.

Quick Fixes

Smart Lighting

Ease of use is a hallmark of universal design. There are inexpensive gadgets that make turning lights on and off anywhere in the house a snap:

• Light switch "extenders" (no wiring required) that place the light switches within easy reach if you're sitting near the switch.

• Tabletop controls for lamps that you can use to turn lamps on by simply touching a 3-inch (7.5 cm) on/off button control sitting on the table, eliminating the need to reach up to turn a switch.

This convenient, hands-free light sensor turns on a designated table lamp when you pass through its detection range. Mount it on a wall or simply place it in an unobtrusive spot on a table or bookcase.

Night-lights are an essential part of healthy living. They protect you and your family from nighttime accidents.

Removing a wall or even part of it can dramatically increase the usability of a home. For example, a kitchen wall cut-out provides an extra countertop to eat on or serve from. And while renovating, enlarge the doorways for enhanced accessibility. A combination of ceiling, floor, and table lamps, along with natural lighting, creates a well-lit room.

IT'S WISE TO BE SAFE

Dim It Down

In certain situations, too much light can be a problem. If you have a lot of natural light coming in your windows, this can create glare that can make it difficult to see well. Control glare by adding blinds or by hanging awnings outside.

easy to go green
Light It Up!

Making improvements to your overall lighting is one of the easiest ways to go green. It'll save you money on your energy bills, and you'll feel good about reducing pollution and greenhouse gasses. Here are three easy ways to help the planet and your pocketbook at the same time.

1. Update your old fixtures with energy-efficient ones. They'll distribute light more efficiently and give a higher quality light output. Look for the Energy Star label on a variety of stylish designs, from table and floor lamps to hardwired options, such as front porch and ceiling lights.

2. Use daylight. Take advantage of nature's free stuff and let daylight penetrate your home's interior. Open your shades and blinds to flood your rooms with daylight (just not on hot sunny days). Need a modicum of privacy? Use sheer curtains where needed.

3. Use light colors on the walls, floors, and ceilings to help reduce your electrical use: they reflect more light than dark colors.

easy to go green
Purchasing Tips for CFLs

Long lasting. Make sure to invest in good quality lightbulbs, as less expensive ones don't last as long and give inferior light.

Color. For general light, choose a lightbulb that has a color temperature between 2700K and 3000K and a color-rendering index (CRI) of at least 80. Often these bulbs are referred to as "warm white" or "white." For close-up work, consider a "daylight" full-spectrum bulb with a minimum color temperature of 5100K and a CRI of at least 91. Look for these numbers on the packaging.

Wattages. Select a CFL that's about one-third the wattage of the incandescent bulb it replaces. For example, a 32-watt CFL is similar to a 100-watt incandescent bulb.

Three-way bulbs. Choose a three-way CFL if you have a lamp with a three-way socket. Otherwise, like incandescent bulbs, it will only light up on the second turn, or the middle position, of the three-way switch.

Dimmable. If you have the lamp on a dimmer switch, make sure to purchase a dimmable CFL. Standard CFLs don't dim. Also, keep in mind that even dimmable CFLs don't dim the way incandescent bulbs do. Most CFLs just dim from a high to a low setting (about half of the high setting); but with incandescent, you have an almost infinite range of light levels, from very dim to bright. Finally, as incandescents dim, the color gets "warmer"; as CFLs dim, their color remains constant, so you won't get a soft glow.

Size. Not all CFLs will fit existing lamps, so make sure they're the right size before you purchase them.

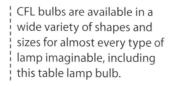

CFL bulbs are available in a wide variety of shapes and sizes for almost every type of lamp imaginable, including this table lamp bulb.

Compact Fluorescent Lightbulbs

CFLs are small-diameter fluorescent bulbs that are available as a screw-in replacement for standard incandescent bulbs. Did you know that if just one room in every U.S. household used Energy Star CFLs, we could keep one trillion pounds of pollution out of our air? Although they cost more than incandescent bulbs, CFLs use 66 percent less energy, resulting in considerable savings over the bulb's lifetime. They also last up to 10 times longer. That means fewer wobbly trips up a ladder for replacement.

Also, CFLs are very different from the fluorescent lightbulbs of the past; gone are the harsh, cold blue tones of the old models. These newer bulbs provide a warm color similar to an incandescent bulb and give off very little heat. However, CFLs do contain small amounts of mercury, so be sure to dispose of them properly. See earth911.com for recycling guidelines in your area.

Good lighting plays a role in preventing accidents. Make sure the kitchen area is well lit with a variety of lighting choices: overhead, under the cabinets, and above the stovetop.

Full-Spectrum Incandescent Lightbulbs

These bulbs duplicate the characteristics of natural daylight. They contain a rare earth element, neodymium, which filters out the yellow in the color spectrum, making colors appear more vibrant. Many eye specialists, aware of this comfortable light quality, commonly recommend full-spectrum bulbs for those sensitive to glare. The lightbulb's shape is very similar to that of the standard incandescent variety, but the neodymium colors the bulb blue when it's unlit. Several major companies manufacture them under different names, but they are described as "daylight bulbs." Although not as energy-efficient as CFLs, they last up to five times longer than standard incandescent bulbs.

Standard Incandescent Lightbulbs

Still the most common lightbulbs used in homes today, the standard incandescent bulb is a real "gas guzzler." Only 10 percent of the electricity it uses actually produces light; the remaining 90 percent just produces heat. Soon incandescent bulbs will become dinosaurs, as consumers throughout the country switch to more efficient lighting as a result of legislation. A new energy bill passed by Congress in 2008 virtually bans incandescent bulbs by 2014 since they no longer meet the new energy-efficiency standards.

Incandescent bulbs are available in various finishes, including clear, frosted, and soft white. The clear finish is harsh on the eyes because it produces a lot of glare; choose a frosted or soft-white finish instead.

Halogen Bulbs

Halogen bulbs are a type of incandescent bulb that has a bright, white light. Some eye specialists recommend this type of light for people with impaired vision, claiming that it increases legibility while reading. But these bulbs burn at very high temperatures and generate a lot of heat, causing discomfort if positioned close to the user's face or body. Moreover, if used incorrectly, halogen bulbs can be a potential fire hazard. Because of these drawbacks, you're better off using an alternative light source.

Lamps

Some lamps are rated to hold only a 60-watt incandescent bulb, and using a higher wattage is a fire hazard. If you don't know your lamp's rating and you need wattage over 60 watts, use a CFL. A 32-watt compact fluorescent bulb gives the same amount of light as a 100-watt incandescent bulb.

LED bulbs for table lamps are now available. They are more energy efficient than flourescent bulbs, contain no mercury, and are dimmable. Though they are expensive, prices are likely to drop in the near future.

The standard light bulb in the American household today will become a relic of the past as new legislation phases out the use of these energy-inefficient bulbs.

Quick Fixes

Installing Outlets on a Budget

Consider the number and types of electrical outlets you'll need for your lighting, entertainment systems, computers, home office, and automated gadgets and systems. Remodeling is a great time to make sure you have enough outlets to meet all your needs. Besides, having more electrical outlets means fewer extension cords across the floor—all too easy to trip over! If you're on a budget, install surface-mounted cable along the baseboard (no need to break open the walls). Mount electrical outlets 18 to 24 inches (46 to 61 cm) above the floor. At those heights, they're easier to reach, whether you're standing or sitting, than the ones located down at the baseboard level.

Windows

In the universal home, windows are a vital element for health and well-being. They connect us to nature and our surroundings, keep out hot or cold weather, allow fresh air in, and help us navigate our interiors with daylight. If you live in an old home with drafty windows, dark interiors, or limited views, or have difficulty opening and closing your windows, there's a lot you can do to fix these problems. Whether you replace your windows or shore up what you have, three things to consider are ease of use, energy efficiency, and daylight.

Ease of Use

Ideally, every room in the house should have at least one window that's easily reached and opened, even if upper-body strength or manual dexterity is limited. Casement windows with a crank or lever mechanism are typically recommended in the universal home: they're relatively easy to open and accessible from a seated position—though they're ill-suited to the installation of window air conditioners. On the other hand, double-hung windows that open from top to bottom can be hard to reach and require more strength to operate. With this type, you may be able to reduce the strength required by loosening the tension screws in the frames with a screwdriver.

Energy Efficiency

If your home has old, single-glazed windows, you're probably wasting a lot of money on needlessly high heating and cooling bills. Swapping out your old windows with today's high-performance thermal windows helps conserve natural resources while offering you many benefits. Thermal windows:

This large expanse of windows provides abundant interior lighting for a kitchen herb garden and beautiful views to the outdoors.

• Reduce your energy bill.

• Keep fabric and carpeting from fading (less ultraviolet light from outside to inside).

• Cut down on glare for more comfortable interior light.

• Have warmer windowpanes that allow you to sit closer to the windows and bask in the winter light.

• Produce less condensation and require less maintenance.

Daylight

If you're like the average person, you spend about 90 percent of your time indoors. Daylight can brighten those indoor spaces, along with your mood, so flood your interiors with as much free, natural light as you can. If overgrown vines or branches shield a window, cut them back to allow more light in.

If you're building an addition, use large, energy-efficient windows with cross-ventilation. Ceiling windows, or skylights, are now virtually leakproof. You can place them in kitchens, bedrooms, even bathrooms—anywhere you want extra natural light and views of the sky. Heat loss or gain can be minimized with integral electronic blinds with timed closing devices or with "switchable" glass that shades itself. In areas where there's not enough space for traditional skylights, such as hallways, solar tubes can be used to create pools of natural illumination.

Eco-friendly windows are now available with decorative features, including between-the-glass grille options. This one has a stylish, curved transom.

easy to go green
Energy-Efficient Windows

Choosing windows today is more of a science than an art because the climate where you live will determine the exact specifications (for example, type of glass, coatings, or hurricane proofing). Before buying, you'll need to learn what kind of window is right for your location. In general, look for the following green features:

• Double-pane windows filled with inert gas (for example, argon)

• Low-emittance (low-E) glass coating that reduces heat loss but allows the room to be warmed by sunshine

• Eco-friendly recycled wood fiber and vinyl composition frame and sash material

Hallways are often dim, hard-to-navigate spaces, but this roomy passageway uses skylights and a glass door to flood the space with natural light. At nighttime, recessed ceiling lights help illuminate the hall.

easy to go green
Six Wintertime Energy-Saving Tips

Here are some easy ways to save on your energy bill:

1. Insulate room air conditioners with covers.

2. Replace screens with storm windows.

3. Put weather-stripping around windows and doorframes that leak air.

4. Seal any holes, cracks, and gaps.

5. Place heat-resistant reflectors between the radiator and walls to heat the room, not the wall.

6. Remove drapes and furniture that block air vents.

Retrofit to Reduce Heat Buildup

One cost-saving approach to improving the thermal properties of your existing windows is to install a solar-control film on them. These thin film coatings absorb or reflect solar energy, screening out the summer sun, and reflecting back escaping heat during the winter. There are many varieties on the market today; choose the lightest film color available (to avoid darkening the interior) that will also absorb substantial heat. Some transparent films have a visible-light transmission of 70 percent, and a 55 percent heat rejection, while blocking 90 percent of the infrared rays responsible for heat buildup. Another option is to use solar shades both to dress a window in clean modern lines *and* to reduce heat buildup.

When replacing your windows, choose low-emittance (low-E) windows for improved energy efficiency. Keeping heat in during the winter and out during the summer helps reduce carbon emissions *and* your monthly electric bills over time. They are available in various styles, including casement windows that open easily with the turn of a lever.

Energy-Efficient Heating & Cooling

In the universal home, individual thermal comfort and energy conservation go hand in hand. If you're planning a large remodeling project, talk with your heating and cooling company about the option of installing separate zone controls in each room. In the long run, this can be an economic and eco-friendly approach.

Gas Heating Systems

Many people consider gas heating systems to be an environmentally friendly energy source, as they burn more cleanly and efficiently than oil and have low emissions at each point along the energy cycle (for example, extraction, processing, delivery, and consumption). But if your heating system was installed more than 25 years ago, it's probably producing pollution and costing you more money to operate than a new energy-efficient model. Replacing it with a new Energy Star gas system will substantially improve the efficiency of your heating system, save you money on energy bills, and reduce your household's environmental impact. To find out what options you have for improving or replacing your current heating and hot water systems, go to energystar.gov. You may also want to consult an expert. Many electric utilities and gas companies offer free home-energy audits, or you can pay a modest amount for an independent audit.

Solar Energy Systems

Solar energy makes use of the abundant energy in the sun. Eco-friendly solar systems offer "free" electricity, though upfront costs are high. However, it's a good idea to see if federal or state tax credits are available for making energy-saving home improvements in your area. Check out energystar.gov for more information.

Heat Your Home Safely
Any fuel-burning furnace can leak carbon monoxide gas into the house under various circumstances. To keep your family and your home healthy, make sure that you:

• Have your system checked periodically by a licensed technician for ventilation problems, faulty connections, or defective parts.

• Have your chimney and flue cleaned every year.

• Install a carbon monoxide detector on each floor of the house.

Quick Fixes

Warm It Up!
Do you have a cold room that you'd like to warm up for a visiting relative on a wintry day? For an easy retrofit, consider radiant ceiling panels, which are much safer than portable room heaters. These unobtrusive, inch-thick panels heat up within minutes and can be operated by a remote switch. There are no moving parts, such as fans or compressors, and they're relatively maintenance-free. Like any type of electric heating device, radiant panels can be expensive to operate, but they can provide supplemental heating when extending your heating system is impractical.

If you're retrofitting your home, consider solar panels for some of your energy needs—and you may be eligible for a green tax credit. Solar energy systems are available in several models, including roof shingles or the more common photovoltaic (PV) panels shown here.

Interior Features That Improve Accessibility

Solar Electricity

If you're retrofitting an older home, you may be able to use solar energy for at least some of your energy needs. Solar systems are available in several models, including the more common photovoltaic (PV) panels or those that look like traditional roof shingles. Mounted on the roof, these glass panels use semiconductor materials to convert sunlight into solar energy. Other features of a PV system include an inverter, which transforms the solar energy into electricity needed to run home appliances, and batteries that store excess energy for use at night or on cloudy, rainy days.

Solar Thermal Hot Water Systems

If you don't want to spring for an entire solar home, but still want to use some solar energy, you can opt for solar hot water. Solar systems can be an efficient way to generate hot water for your home's water heaters, radiant floors, and radiators. Such a system usually includes storage tanks and solar collectors, which can be placed on the roof, side by side or under the PV panels. Solar water heating systems cost more to purchase and install than conventional water heating systems, but they usually save you money in the long run. The U.S. Department of Energy tells us that on average, water-heating bills should drop 50 to 80 percent after installing a solar water heater.

In the universal home, designers give attention to safe navigation of all living spaces. In this section, we'll explore a variety of interior features that can improve your home's accessibility and make it easier to move about the house.

Using the stairs can be a great form of daily exercise, but make sure they're safe. The universal design staircase has handrails on both sides for added safety. When possible, the treads should be in a different color than the risers to improve visibility.

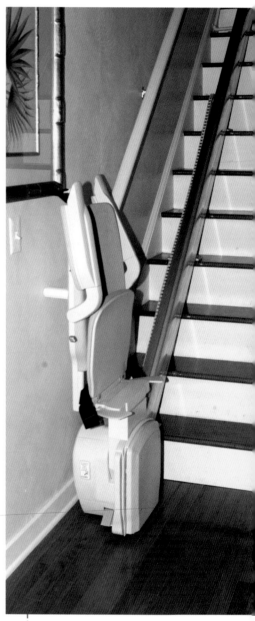

When climbing stairs is no longer a safe option, consider a stair lift. You can rent one for short-term use or purchase one outright for extended independent living. And when the seat is tucked away, others can use the stairs too.

Safer Stairs

Climbing stairs offers a readily available form of daily exercise, but falling down them is the cause of a great number of injuries in people of all ages. That's why stairs in the universal home have enhanced safety features, along with alternative methods for moving from floor to floor, such as chair lifts, elevators, and one-story living.

Here are four stair-related things to consider that can make your stairs safer for everyone.

1. Handrails

The universal staircase has round handrails that are 1½ inches (4 cm) in diameter on both sides of the stairs. Handrails on both sides offer tremendous help with balance and are user-friendly for anyone, but especially for individuals who have limited strength on one side. This simple addition can sometimes make all the difference in a person's ability to climb stairs as long as they're still mobile. The rails should be securely anchored into wall studs to support the user's full weight, extend 12 inches (30.5 cm) from the top and bottom of the stairs, measure 33 to 36 inches (84 to 91.5 cm) from the stair tread, and be 1½ inches (4 cm) away from the wall. If young children live with you, consider installing a lower handrail for their use.

2. Stair Materials

There's no documentation showing that one type of flooring material for stairs is safer than another, but we do know that a matte finish on wood or stone steps is essential for fall prevention. If you're considering carpeting the stairs, tightly woven carpet or a dense cut pile is the wisest choice.

3. Light & Color

It's important that you and your guests can visually distinguish one step from the next. First of all, light all stairs well, particularly the top and bottom stair. You also may want to highlight the step's edge by painting a 1- to 2-inch (2.5 to 5 cm) bright, colorful stripe along the edge of each tread. (Yes, you can even paint a stripe directly on the edges of carpet.) Or if you're installing new carpet or building stairs, consider using two different colors of carpet or wood on the risers and on the treads.

4. Risers

Open risers, which have a vertical opening between the steps, can be particularly dangerous, because it's easy to get your toe caught when climbing up the stairs. To protect against trips and falls, close these openings.

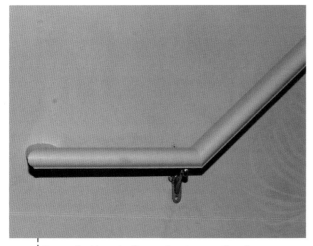

Extended handrails can improve safety because they offer a handhold for stabilizing your balance at the top and bottom of the stairs.

Highlighting the edge of each step with a darker border is a smart idea. It helps you easily identify each step and makes for surer footing.

Home Elevators

If one-story living isn't convenient for your household, and you have a healthy budget, a home elevator may be the right choice for you. There are several models to consider, depending on available floor space, design preference, and cost. As this is a big-ticket purchase, try to go for a "test drive" at a manufacturer's showroom to evaluate individual features, such as noise level, ease of use, and comfort of ride.

If you're building a new home or addition, keep this in mind: it's much easier and less expensive to install an elevator during construction, as shafts can be economically included. You can even stack up closet space (your future shaft) floor-to-floor that can be retrofitted with an elevator if you need one in the future.

The three elevator models described below offer an emergency backup lowering system so you'll never be stranded between floors during a power outage.

1. Freestanding Elevator Cab

This no-frills elevator is the least expensive model. It doesn't require a shaft or machine room, just a floor cutout for the cab to pass through and a load-bearing wall on which to mount the steel tracks it rides on. Depending on the model, these wheelchair-accessible elevators can carry 450 to 500 pounds (204 to 227 kg) and move a distance of 16 or 23 feet (5 or 7 m). If you prefer a bit more style, choose a custom upgrade that makes it look

This stylish home elevator provides accessibility in a two- or three-story home while blending in seamlessly with the home's décor.

This freestanding glass and metal elevator is as functional as it is beautiful. Wheelchair-accessible, this sculptural cab maximizes living space since it doesn't require a pit or a machine room, only a reinforced wall for the rail and a floor cutout. Its glass windows allow light and views.

more like a traditional elevator at a fraction of the cost.

2. Freestanding Glass & Metal Elevator

If you're looking for more drama and pizzazz, chose the freestanding glass and metal cube-style elevator. Used by luxury hotels to wow their riders with panoramic views, this elevator cab is pneumatically powered. Like its less expensive cousin, it doesn't require a shaft or machine room—just a floor cutout for the cab to pass through. Some models carry up to 550 pounds (249.5 kg), move a distance of 30 feet (9 m), and are wheelchair-accessible. This attractive elevator will cost you, but it's well worth the expense if you have the budget.

3. Hydraulic Elevator

If you're building a new home, have available floor space, a sizable budget, and traditional taste, the luxury hydraulically powered elevator is your best bet. This style elevator is the one we're all familiar with and offers many custom features, including wood-panel interiors, quiet operation, and room for several passengers. It does, however, require a shaft, a machine room, and an excavated pit; hence, the extra expense. In some situations, it may be more economical to house the elevator in a small addition along the outside of the house, especially if the elevator serves more than two floors.

Flooring

Your choice of flooring adds to a room's drama and style, and, what's more important, it impacts your health, safety, and comfort. For example, allergies, falls, noise levels, and even your degree of comfort while walking, cooking, or showering are all influenced by the type of flooring you have. In the universal home, flooring materials are easy to walk and wheel on; have a matte, unpolished finish; contribute to good indoor air quality; and are level throughout the home. Consider the following flooring choices; they're all eco-friendly with built-in safety. Keep in mind that lighter-colored floors will make spaces seem larger—a real plus in a smaller room.

Wall-to-Wall Carpeting

Today's carpeting is available in a variety of textures, fiber compositions, and colors. If you're concerned about indoor air quality or have allergies, make sure to specify carpeting that doesn't have any chemical treatments, such as permanent stain resistance, mothproofing, or anti-microbial agents (fungicides). Dense, low-pile carpet is a smart choice; it makes movement easy, absorbs sound, reduces heat loss, and cushions a fall. Wool carpet is an environmentally responsible choice (although it costs more), as it's made from a renewable resource, is durable and biodegradable. Wool is also flame-resistant—an added benefit. Choose a thin, not a plush, padding since it provides a more stable floor surface (your foot won't "sink" into it as easily).

When choosing carpeting, look for a dense, tight weave that's easy to both walk and wheel over. Lighter colors make any room look larger. A small pindot pattern hides dirt marks. Carpeting also helps to absorb background noises.

Wood Floors

Make sure all your wood floors have a matte finish—the floors will be less slippery and reflect less glare. Wood floors with area rugs can be visually stunning, but they can cause falls, especially for those with mobility impairments, so use area rugs with caution. They'll be safer if you securely fasten them to the floor with two-sided tape or place a nonslip liner underneath.

If you're installing new flooring, consider using wood from sustainable forests. Bamboo is an excellent flooring choice; this fast-growing tree is easily renewable. And it's available in over 50 different water-based stains, so you won't have to sacrifice style for this eco-friendly flooring choice. Other sustainable woods include heart pine and Southern yellow pine, available in country style, 10-inch (25.5 cm) planks. Or if you like more of an antique look, consider the rich patina of reclaimed wood from older homes.

This marble floor tile has a matte, user-friendly, nonglare surface. Stone flooring, however, poses a challenge for some if they need to stand for extended periods. Consider wood or carpeting if you have leg issues that require a more forgiving surface.

Ceramic Tiles

Another popular flooring choice is ceramic tile, especially for the foyer, kitchen, and bathroom. You'll want to find the least slippery tile, and this quality is measured by the "coefficient of friction," or COF. A high COF, 0.6 or higher, is generally a safe, slip-resistant floor. If you're doing a major renovation, consider installing a radiant heat floor—you'll never have to walk barefoot on cold tile again.

This beautiful, easy-to-maintain wood floor has a slip-resistant matte finish. When refinishing wood flooring, use eco-friendly water-based stains with no or low VOCs (volatile organic compounds).

easy to go green
Wall-to-Wall Carpet

• Choose felt padding over plastic or synthetic rubber padding.

• Look for wool or recycled carpeting.

• Use tack-down installations, not glue, as adhesives can emit volatile organic compounds (VOCs), and you can partially recycle the carpeting when removed.

• Recycle your old carpeting. Each year, five billion pounds of carpet are thrown away, most of it winding up in landfills. Manufacturers can reuse your spent carpeting by putting it back into new carpet and carpet-related products.

Resource: Earth Weave Carpet Mills (earthweave.com)

IT'S WISE TO BE SAFE

Floors

For those who walk slowly or with difficulty, moving from one flooring surface to another may contribute to falls. The use of one flooring material for all rooms throughout the house—other than for bathrooms and kitchens—is preferable.

Sheet Flooring

Sheet flooring, especially linoleum, is another wise flooring choice, since it's easily cleaned and softer underfoot than ceramic tile. Linoleum, made primarily from linseed oil, pine tree resins, cork, and chalk, uses renewable resources and offers durability without compromising aesthetics. Available in a wide array of colors and mottled patterns, linoleum costs more than low-cost vinyl flooring, but its durability makes its life-cycle costs lower.

Doors, Doorways, & Hallways

The universal home is designed to be accessible to people of all ages—to the maximum extent possible. It has wider doorways so that if you, a family member, or a friend uses a large mobility device, your home will still be accessible and welcoming. Ideally, the perfect time to enlarge all your doorways is during a renovation; interior door openings should have a minimum 36 inches (91.5 cm) of clear space. This width not only creates an aesthetically pleasing elegance and grace, but it's a practical advantage

This light-filled hallway has abundant lighting from multiple sources, including skylights, ceiling down lights, and wall sconces. The no-threshold doorway allows for easy, safe passage.

Universal design flooring is good for everyone, young and old. This slip-resistant, resilient flooring is easy to maintain, eco-friendly, and easy on the knees. The inset colored diamond adds a lively note.

This spacious doorway makes passing between rooms effortless. The flush entryway increases safety since there's no threshold to trip over.

when you're moving furniture or carrying packages. If the door openings aren't easily enlarged in your home, replace the existing hinges with "swing clear" hinges and remove the bottom doorstops, if needed. You'll gain up to 3 inches (7.5 cm): that may be enough to get larger pieces of furniture through unscathed or to avoid scraped elbows if you or a guest uses a mobility device. And don't forget to widen the hallways as well; you'll want passageways that are at least 42 inches (107 cm) wide instead of the more typical 36 inches (91.5 cm).

Doors

If you're replacing some of your interior doors, consider whether some transitional spaces really need any door at all. Perhaps you can just hang a curtain instead. If, however, you need new doors for privacy or to conserve energy, there are several companies that manufacture eco-friendly universal doors, complete with beautiful details and attractive moldings.

Doorknobs

Anyone can achieve an important universal design feature by replacing round doorknobs with European-style lever handles that are attractive and easier to use. They're available in a variety of decorative styles, including swirling curved handles and elegant antique finishes. And for increased visibility, color-contrast the lever handle with the door. At some point, you also might want to add a sec-

Quick Fixes

Wheelchairs & Doorways

You can replace a wheelchair that can't fit through doorways with a narrow transport wheelchair, if your situation is temporary or it's not possible to change the doorway width. This type of narrow wheelchair (19 to 24 inches [48 to 61 cm] wide) will fit through most doorways. The trade-off, though, is that it can't be self-propelled—someone else will need to push it.

Spacious doorways with flush thresholds let everyone move through living spaces with greater ease. Larger door openings also allow more light to flow through adjacent rooms and visually connect the spaces.

Smart-Home Technologies

This stylish lever door handle requires little effort to use.

ond door handle placed in the center of the door to allow for easier access from a seated position.

Doorsills Be Gone

Doorsills are tripping hazards for anyone, but especially for those who walk with a shuffle. They're also difficult to wheel over for someone using a walker or a wheelchair. Whenever possible, remove doorsills to create a smooth floor surface between rooms; or at least install a beveled strip or a threshold ramp.

easy to go green
Doors

When buying a new door, look for:

• Recovered and recycled wood fibers

• No formaldehyde

• Low-emitting adhesives

Smart-home technologies are no longer the stuff of science fiction, nor are they found only in the homes of the rich and famous. Basically, a smart system is anything that lets you automatically control your home's devices and systems, everything from your stove to your entire heating and cooling system.

Smart-home technology ranges from the simple and the inexpensive to the pricier and much more complex. At the most basic level, you can get stand-alone systems for individual controls. For instance, you could use a simple remote on a key chain to turn on interior lights from the outside. Or you can purchase packages for the whole house that can manage lighting, climate control, computer networking, security, watering systems, and entertainment.

If you have a whole-house system, your computer and all of the various systems, appliances, and other devices in your house are connected together by means of cables or wireless links. Load the necessary software onto your computer and add a high-speed Internet connection, and you're ready to control virtually everything in your home from anywhere in your house—or anywhere in the world. So, for example, right before you leave the house, you could simply activate your smart-home system instead of racing around the house doing those last-minute checks. The system would automatically take care of turning off all the lights (except those in the foyer, so

An open kitchen and dining plan offers a wide circulation area and unobstructed access to all the people in the home, whether they're cooking in the spacious kitchen or relaxing nearby. A quiet range hood enhances everyone's ability to communicate.

you can see where you're going), turning down the thermostat, arming the security system, setting the sprinkler timers, and making sure all cooking appliances are off.

In short, smart features offer convenience and enhanced safety, making it easier to control your environment and provide security, all with a push of a button. Specifically, such systems can:

• Reduce the level of physical activity needed to maintain your home; what may be a convenience feature now may become a necessity in the future.

• Reduce the number of things you need to do every day. That's helpful if you're busy, forgetful, or have a cognitive impairment.

• Reduce energy costs—you can save 30 to 50 percent on water costs and up to 20 percent on energy.

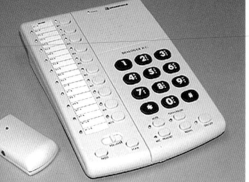

Smart-home products include a wireless doorbell signaler that lets you know someone is at the door even if you're in the back of the house and a voice-activated phone that requires minimal physical effort.

Look for These Smart-System Features

If you love your independence, smart systems can help you stay in control of your environment. Technology, however, should simplify your life, not make it more complicated! When looking for a separate unit or a whole-house system that's right for you, look for the following universal design features: easy to program, easy to maintain, and easy to use.

Smart systems usually require a steep learning curve, but careful product selection can make learning easier. First of all, you'll want to consider an interface that you're comfortable with—some systems offer access through more than one interface, including a computer monitor, a wall panel (keypad or touch screen), a handheld device, the telephone, the Internet, or even the sound of your voice. Once the system is programmed, you'll want the easiest-to-read interface. Look for models with large buttons with more space between them (to avoid pushing the wrong button) and large fonts for easier reading. And if your vision is significantly impaired, check out the models that include a 17-inch (43 cm) touch panel with buttons the size of a pack of cards.

Many systems use existing electrical wires; some are wireless. But if you're doing extensive renovations, consider running state-of-the art wiring (right now, it's category 5 cable) to all locations where you might eventually want a keypad or touch panel installed. Running conduit to create a path for additional wires for future technology is also a good idea.

How to Start

The three most frequently requested smart-home systems are lighting, temperature control, and security. You can get whole-house systems or stand-alone units for frequently used rooms—without spending a fortune. Throughout the book, I'll be discussing a variety of smart options that can simplify your life and help you and family members maintain independence. But if you're considering a complex whole-house system, consult with a home-automation specialist to learn about the best systems for your lifestyle and needs.

Easy Smart Lighting

Here are two simple, stand-alone smart products that will make lighting up your home easy and efficient.

1. Occupancy sensor light switches can be used throughout the house or just in the rooms you use the most. You can install these affordable, hands-free devices without new wiring. The sensor switch detects movement and turns the lights on automatically as you enter a room, certainly a convenience feature when your arms are laden with groceries. And the switch helps to save energy—it turns off the lights automatically when the room isn't in use. However, if you're sitting still, you'll need to move every so often for the sensor light to detect your presence.

2. Handheld lighting remotes are the easiest solution. Would you like to put your feet up and control the lights from your favorite chair or from your bedside table? If you're looking for an easy-to-use wireless smart system, this device is for you. The "receiver" plugs into any standard outlet; you simply plug the lamp into the receiver and your handheld remote control is ready to turn your lights on or off. This device is handy if you appreciate convenience, but it's a necessity if you

A remote video system gives you vital information at a glance. It can be indispensable when living alone. For example, if you're recovering from surgery, this system lets you see who's at the door—and you can buzz them in without leaving the room.

Smart technology allows you to control your environment with push button ease. Monitoring systems and products that adjust lighting levels and automate your thermostat are just a few examples of smart technology that simplify and enrich everyday living.

have a serious mobility impairment. The affordable remote is available at most home stores; you can always purchase several if you want to control more than one lamp.

Heating & Cooling

Today's energy-efficient systems give you individual thermostatic control of the room or rooms where you spend time. A smart thermostat allows you to program your furnace or central air conditioning system so you can get the right temperature at the right time of day. Here's a typical winter weekday schedule: at 10:00 P.M the temperature is automatically lowered, but the room is warm and cozy again when you awake at 6:00 A.M. The smart thermostat lowers the temperature again when you go off to work, but is programmed to give you a warm welcome upon your return.

Security

Smart technologies can provide the kind of security we want at any age. For example, your automated security system detects an intruder. Although it's certainly a stressful event, your smart system helps protect you by flashing all your lights, sounding the alarm, and sending an alert to the police or a local security firm.

These systems also afford a slightly different type of security that becomes increasingly important as we age. Let's say that a family member needs some extra monitoring for health reasons. You can install a stand-alone smart system unit that sends a message to your cell phone, alerting you that the temperature in his or her home dropped too low or that the person hasn't opened a pillbox at a designated time. You can act immediately, intervening before a

real crisis develops. These systems are relatively affordable, and there are no monthly fees; their installation is similar to that of an answering machine.

There are also more sophisticated all-inclusive monitoring systems that operate by sensing motion in the various rooms of the dwelling; there are no video cameras, so it's not overly intrusive. After establishing a baseline for a person's normal daily habits, the company sends telephone alerts to you if there are deviations in the individual's schedule, such as his or her morning rising time, meal times, bathroom usage, or medication schedule. Costs include the initial purchase price, which can vary widely, as well as a monthly fee.

Gallery

Open, free-flowing spaces create accessibility for everyone; if you or a loved one needed a mobility device, your home would still be usable.

Living rooms with both natural and interior lighting, a warm hearth, and comfortable seating offer gracious living at any age.

A skylight floods this bathroom with natural light while sconces flanking the mirror help light the sink area. If you or a loved one has low vision, consider fabric shades that hide the light source instead of glass globes.

CHAPTER 4

Entryways, Gardens,
& the Outdoors

Enjoying the outdoors is one of life's greatest pleasures—and it's good for you, too. The healing qualities of nature promote well-being and relaxation: keys to a healthy lifestyle.

In most standard homes, though, entryways, exterior stairs, and uneven walkways can make getting outside and moving around outdoors an exasperating challenge. The universal home, on the other hand, has accessible entrances and gardens so people of all ages and abilities can delight in nature and safely appreciate its benefits.

From sprucing up a deck to building a garden patio, this chapter features design ideas that can enhance your time outdoors.

No-Hassle Entryways

The ability to come and go as we please is a freedom most of us take for granted. Even if climbing stairs isn't a problem for you at this point, the unpredictability of life means things won't always stay this way. That's why it's important for your home to have at least one accessible entryway. In this section, we'll explore a variety of ways to create a no-step entrance, including sloped pathways, landscaped ramps, as well as porch and stair lifts. We'll also discuss universal design practices that can increase the safety and usability of your existing stairs.

You can make getting in and out of your home easier by placing an inclined threshold ramp at the door. This weather-resistant rubber ramp is available in several heights and widths for different doorway sizes.

This universal design entryway is welcoming to all with a level walkway and an accessible no-step entrance.

Sloping Pathways

If you're remodeling, talk to your architect about designing a sloping no-step entryway. Slope the land up to the doorway and line the pathway with flowering plants and shrubs. The easiest slope for walking or wheeling is 1 inch (2.5 cm) of rise for every 20 inches (51 cm) of walkway. Depending on how the home is sited, you'll need to make sure the slope is sufficient to drain water properly.

Ramps

Contrary to popular belief, ramps can look great and preserve the style of your home. For a seamless, stylish look, border the ramp with small trees and planter boxes filled with flowers, and integrate decorative details from your porch railing and balustrade into the ramp's design.

Ramps, however, aren't suitable for every person or house. Some people with balance problems prefer using stairs—so make sure your stairs pass the safety test (see page 68). And not every home has the space for a ramp, especially in urban areas. Very long ramps can be unsightly, so the

This attractive cement walkway slopes toward the doorway and is tinted with a soft adobe color that blends in beautifully with the landscape.

Although the most popular ramps are made of wood or concrete, there may be times when a portable or modular metal ramp is preferable. Lining the entire ramp with plantings and flowers will create a more seamless design.

rule of thumb is: if your stairs are over 30 inches (76 cm) high, install a porch or stair lift instead (see page 67).

Below are some general tips for adding a ramp to your home. Check to see if you need a building permit, as some communities do require one. Of course, you'll also want to consult an experienced builder to be sure the dimensions, materials, and design will work for your home, climate, and lifestyle.

Slope of Ramp

Although building codes allow ramps to be built with a slope of 1 inch (2.5 cm) for every 12 inches (30.5 cm) in length, wheeling someone up or down a ramp this steep takes considerable strength; plus, a wheelchair can roll out of control, or you can injure your back pushing someone up an incline. A slope of 1 inch (2.5 cm) for every 20 inches (51 cm) in length is easier to use, but better suited to a one-step entrance.

Length of Ramp

You can build long ramps in an L-shape or a switchback pattern; these designs have a run of ramp and then a

An Atlanta affiliate of the Georgia Habitat for Humanity has pledged to build all their homes with accessible entrances and has now built 950+ new homes with gently sloping ramps.

90° or a 180° turn, followed by another run of ramp. Very long ramps are less attractive and more impractical than short ones. If your setback or your lot slope requires such a long ramp, consider a location less prominent than the front of the house, if possible.

Materials for Ramp

Let personal style, safety, and ease of maintenance guide your decisions when choosing the ramp's materials.

• Treated wood requires annual sealing or painting. Use paint that dries to a nonslip, textured finish (due to the addition of sandy grit) to avoid cracking, warping, and mold.

• Composite wood products require no maintenance (such as annual painting or sealing) and are available in beautiful patterns and weathered finishes. Made of recycled materials—such as plastics, scrap wood, or sawdust—without any chemical preservatives, the surfaces are pebbly textured and slip-resistant. Initially more expensive than treated wood, composite products may be less expensive in the long run because there are no annual maintenance costs.

This wooden ramp is built with a gentle, safe slope. A covered gazebo offers both shade and a playful ambience.

This wooden ramp—placed on the side of the home and wrapping around to the front—uses decorative design details including posts and finials to blend in with the home's design for a residential ambiance.

• Portable metal ramps are manufactured in sections, easily installed, and ideal in certain situations. For example, you can use a short portable metal ramp for a one- or two-step apartment entrance, and then tuck it away when no longer needed. You can temporarily use a longer metal ramp at your front or side door to allow a parent (who can't climb stairs) to easily come and go while recuperating after surgery in your first-floor den.

For more information on building a wooden ramp for your home, refer to the Center for Universal Design's online manual "Wood Ramp Design: How to Add a Ramp That Looks Good and Works Too" (design.ncsu.edu/cud/pubs_p/docs/rampbooklet296 final.pdf).

Porch & Stair Lifts

There are several types of electric lifts that raise a standing or a seated person onto a porch when stair climbing is no longer an option. For wheelchair users who can't easily transfer, you'll want a wheelchair lift that allows the person to remain seated during transit. When looking for a lift that's right for your situation, buy the best you can afford; a quality lift should require only minimal maintenance. And, of course, talk to the dealer about specific space requirements for the type of lift you're considering, including the minimum-size porch landing needed.

Stairways

Not all homes are well situated for a sloped pathway, so if you or your guests climb stairs, you'll want the safest stairs possible. We all know the serious consequences of climbing stairs in the dark, especially if they're slippery or without handrails. You can be seriously injured falling down stairs, so stair safety is a key element of the universal home.

Quick Fixes

No-Cost Ramps
Explore no-cost funding and labor sources, such as local churches or civic organizations, for installing a ramp.

For homes with many steps, use an electric lift to create a no-step entryway. You may want an enclosed model if you live in a place with frequent bad weather.

Stair Safety Test

When conducting your exterior-stair safety test, start by reviewing Safer Stairs in chapter 2 (see page 25). Then answer the following questions as you decide what features to improve.

1. Are your handrails the right length?   Yes ☐ No ☐

You need to extend the handrails on both sides into the landing area; they provide stability and help you balance once you're on the landing.

2. Are the treads/steps nonslip and in good condition?   Yes ☐ No ☐

Falls can happen easily if your foot gets caught on a small crack or if you slip on wet leaves or ice. Repair broken or loose bricks, stones, or cement, so no one has a preventable fall. To help keep your steps ice-free, trim nearby tree branches to maximize the sunlight melting the ice, and keep a good broom and a box of rock salt handy. For enhanced safety in snowy climates, consider a heated rubber front-door mat and stair treads (plugs into a standard 120 V or 240 V outlet) that help melt snow and ice.

3. Are the risers closed?   Yes ☐ No ☐

You can easily catch your feet in open risers (the vertical section supporting a step) when you're climbing the stairs, so close them off.

4. Is there good lighting on the stairs and landing?   Yes ☐ No ☐

Climbing stairs in the dark is dangerous for anyone, so good lighting is a must. Make sure the stairs and the landing have even lighting; shadows can be confusing, especially on stairs. Depending on the design of your porch, consider sconces on both sides of the door, an overhead canopy light, and lights on or along the steps. A relatively new type of stair light installs directly into the stair's risers or along the sidewall of each step. Before buying, you'll want to check to see if these lights can be installed in your existing stairs.

Stair lights are now available with integrated open-patterned risers that allow abundant light to pass through. Choose a simple pattern, especially for individuals with low vision or dementia.

How did you score on the Stair Safety Test? This is one test you really do want to ace! If you checked "no" to any of the questions, take action now to fix the problem.

Using color to boost visibility is an important universal design feature. This decorative staircase, with a dark tread and light riser, makes it easier for everyone, including persons with low vision, to see each step.

One of universal design's goals is to improve safety without sacrificing style. Climbing stairs at night can be made safer with a mix of lighting fixtures, including these risers with built-in eco-friendly lights. If you have low vision, choose a simple pattern.

New Stairs

If you're installing new stairs, design them to be uniform in height and without nosing (a rounded projecting edge on the treads). With nosing, it's too easy to get your foot caught when climbing. Also, install stairs that have closed risers.

If you use a walker, you may find a 4-inch (10 cm) riser height easier for maneuvering than the standard 7-inch (18 cm) height. Similarly, a wider tread—18 to 34 inches (46 to 86.5 cm), instead of the standard 11 inches (28 cm)—will allow the base of the walker to rest on a single stair. Check with an occupational therapist, who can offer other useful design suggestions, especially for accommodating walkers on stairs.

Front Porch

A front porch is a great place to sit and relax, engage with the world outside, or visit with friends and family. It also serves the practical purpose of providing shelter in stormy weather when you're searching for your keys or on a snowy evening when visitors ring the bell.

Rocking chairs and a swinging bench provide for relaxation and ease, especially when overlooking a landscaped garden. Handrails on the stairs and a ramp added to the side of the home would enhance safety and accessibility.

easy to go green
Energy-Efficient Porch Sconces

If you're in the market for new porch lighting, choose Energy Star sconces. These energy-efficient lights automatically turn on when darkness falls and off at dawn. You can choose from hundreds of styles. It's a good idea to select frosted instead of clear glass shades for visual comfort at nighttime.

If buying new sconces isn't in your budget, you can, for about what you'd spend on a lunch out, transform your existing sconces into "smart" lights by simply inserting a photocell sensor into the lamp's socket. Voilà! Your lights will now automatically turn on at dusk and off at dawn.

Depending on the size of your home, you may need nighttime lighting by the walkways, in the garden, and of course, on the stairs and porch. To reduce glare and discomfort, choose frosted instead of clear glass bulbs.

The ideal porch is wide enough to hold several chairs and a table, plus extra seating for visitors. Porch screens are essential in some climates if the porch is to be used at all on hot evenings. Good lighting on both sides of the porch or under the canopy improves security and nighttime enjoyment, allowing you to read or play cards on a summer evening. A shelf, mounted at roughly the height of your waist outside the front door, provides a convenient ledge when you're trying to juggle groceries and simultaneously unlock the door. You'll want a 5 x 5-foot (1.5 x 1.5 m) space outside the entrance door and at least 2 feet (61 cm) on the latch side of the door to allow wheelchairs or scooters to maneuver.

Exterior Doors

All exterior doors should measure 36 inches (91.5 cm) wide to provide easy access (and no-hassle furniture deliveries). Entry doors are available in wood, metal, and fiberglass-composite materials. In a 2004 Consumer Reports test, fiberglass-composite doors received better overall ratings than wood or steel. They have the added benefits of foam insulation and low maintenance. You can treat these composite doors with a wood-grain finish to simulate the look of expensive carpentry. Consider nonbreakable side glass panels, which let additional daylight into the entry hall and allow you to see who's at the door. When using a no- or low-threshold (¼ to ½ inch [6 to 13 mm]) doorway, an automatic drop-bottom seal offers the best protection to keep out water.

A wide entrance and sliding patio doors are available with integrated flush thresholds that ensure easy and safe access.

IT'S WISE TO BE SAFE

Warm Houses for Health
If you have a household member who is frail—who appears weak or tired and walks with uncertainty in his or her step—it's especially important to weatherize exterior doors and windows and use storm windows. Homes with a temperature of 60°F to 65°F (16°C to 18°C) can cause that individual to become ill or experience hypothermia (dangerously low body temperature, below 96°F [36°C]).

Locks

When purchasing new locks for your house and garage doors, buy the best you can afford, since they offer better protection. You'll want deadbolts on all outside doors for higher security. A smart option is an electronic locking system that is operated with a key, card, or touch-control pad. An electronic system offers the additional advantage of a video hookup, allowing you to see who's at the door and to buzz the person in without going to the door.

Doorbells

It's essential to have a doorbell that can be heard from anywhere in the house. You can install several plug-in chimes around the house, upstairs and down.

Address Plaque

A lighted address plaque is both a convenience and a safety feature because it helps visitors and emergency workers easily find their way to your home at night. For simplicity, choose an easy-to-install solar- or battery-powered plaque, and mount it on your porch or mailbox.

The Garage

An electronic garage-door opener that turns on the light when you open the door is an enjoyable luxury for all drivers, but it can be essential for older adults. You'll also want good outdoor light around the entire garage-door area, including the footpath leading to the front and back house doors.

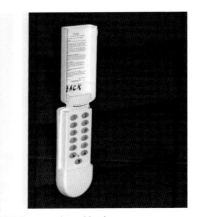

With a touchpad lock, you never have to worry about losing your keys or fumbling for them in the dark. This keyless deadbolt lock system also allows you to control who enters your home. You can change the entry number whenever needed. It could be an impediment, though, to people with memory problems.

This wide doorway welcomes friends and family members of all abilities, and the unbreakable glass panels on either side offer lighting and security benefits. The expansive front porch and bright sconces create an inviting entrance.

Quick Fixes

Maximizing Your Hearing

If you have a hearing impairment, consider installing in one or more rooms flashing lights that blink when anyone rings the bell. If you have only modest hearing loss, a wireless chiming doorbell is a good option. Place the transmitter at the front door and then attach the chime to the wall in the kitchen, den, or bedroom.

Outdoor Spaces

Living well in your own home depends on good design for both indoor and outdoor spaces. Accessibility and comfort are also essential universal features for decks, patios, walkways, and gardens. For example, wheelchair and walker-friendly patio surfaces and color-contrasting pathway borders are easier for all to use. So if you want to reap the proven benefits of enjoying the world of nature right outside your own door, read on!

Decks

Most decks are built adjacent to the house, with sliding doors connecting them to the interior. Depending upon your site, it's also possible to build a low-level deck, raised only slightly off the ground, with a gentle sloping ramp for access. Here are four considerations to help you design a great deck.

1. Best location. Consider orientation for sun and best view.

2. Size. You'll need space for outdoor lounge chairs and side tables, a grill, and a table for family eating; also make sure you have ample room for any mobility devices.

3. Materials. The same considerations appropriate to wooden ramps apply to decks (see page 66).

4. Building codes. Understand building codes in your area before you plan your deck's railing, and make sure the contractor is knowledgeable about what is involved in building a safe deck. The perimeter of a deck can be artfully landscaped with planter boxes, but even this design feature may be regulated by code, so check before you build.

Patios

Patios are wonderful outdoor spaces, and when properly designed they can also feel intimate, even when they open out onto a large yard. You can

Accessible entrances can be achieved in a variety of ways. For example, this attractive cement walkway slopes toward the doorway.

This accessible outdoor deck offers comfortable seating, sun protection, and deck materials that are easy to maintain.

create this coziness by adding "living walls" of trellised plants or flowering shrubs. Depending on how the patio is sited, you may want to add a roof overhang or an arbor that gives you a choice of shade or full sun.

In climates where outdoor living is problematic, an indoor patio is a wise substitute; large windows and skylights can create a room that is as light and airy as the outdoors. If you want to use an indoor patio or sunroom all year round, be sure to have adequate climate controls. Tinted windows will reduce glare, and outdoor awnings will shade the windows from bright summer sun. While manual awnings can be difficult to roll up and down, an electrically operated one can be as easy as turning on a light switch. Check building codes for lot restrictions and also check for underground utilities before starting any construction.

These French doors with a low threshold visually connect the dining room to the outdoors without impeding movement. A covered patio is a welcome relief from the sun or rain, and a pull-down screen protects against insects on muggy evenings. Cushioned chairs are an inviting retreat.

A screened porch offers enjoyment of the outdoors—even on sunny days. A ceiling fan on hot days cools the air by several degrees.

Most outdoor patio floors are either brick or cement. Choose a smooth surface material over handmade tiles, rocks, or granite, as a non-uniform surface can be challenging to walk or wheel on. For an outdoor patio, choose bricks that are right for your climate, or else they'll crack from freezing and thawing.

Concrete can be a good choice, with far more imaginative textures and colors than you might realize. Sandblasting or troweling the top layer can create a slightly textured surface that can minimize slipping but won't impede a mobility device. To color concrete, you can either mix pigment into the entire batch of dry white cement or color just

the top inch. Pastels or adobe-type colors are especially attractive.

If you're building your patio so that it adjoins your living room or another room in the house, specify a sill that is no higher than ¼ inch (6 mm), which can easily accommodate a sliding glass door and allow easy access for walkers or scooters.

This lovely, accessible entrance features an outdoor seating area. The side arms on the weather-resistant wood furniture make it easy to get in and out, while the cushions provide extra comfort. The overhead trellis provides partial shade and welcome relief from the sun on a hot day.

Pathways & Walkways

If you're fortunate enough to have the space for walkways in your garden, a smooth, even surface is your best choice. Colorful flowers bordering the walkway add visual beauty while clearly marking the edges, a thoughtful design detail for those with low vision.

Walkways should be a minimum of 3 feet (91.5 cm) wide, but a wider path—48 to 54 inches (1 to 1.5 m)—gives two people the opportunity to walk side by side. If the weather in your area is often rainy or icy, take care when selecting flooring for the walkways. Colored concrete, brick, or wood composite, with small spaces left between boards to facilitate drainage, are good

This level walkway provides safe footing, and the contrasting color of the grass makes the pathway easier to distinguish in the daytime for those with vision loss. Solar or low voltage lights lining the walkway would further enhance nighttime safety.

choices. As patches of snow and ice can be slippery to walk on, consider a UL-listed heated rubber walkway mat if you live in a cold climate. The mat plugs into a standard 120 V or 240 V outlet, and the manufacturer states that it melts up to 2 inches (5 cm) of snow per hour.

Longevity Essentials

Watching a Flower Grow

Even if your outdoor space is limited, gardening is still an activity you can pursue. There are myriad ways to garden in containers and pots that add beauty to your surroundings. One advantage to container gardening is that small containers are portable; as the seasons change, you can move them to an area that gets the best conditions, thereby extending the growing season. Container gardening also means the end of having to work on your knees.

Planters come in an infinite number of sizes, shapes, and materials; take advantage of this diversity to create a dramatic visual impact. Stone is the most expensive material, but there are many less costly fiberglass imitations that create an almost identical look. Terra-cotta and earthenware pots must be kept dry

Raised beds and planters allow easy access to gardening for people of all ages and abilities, including children and older adults with limited movement. Keep the height within easy reach from a standing or seated position (30 to 33 inches [76.2 to 83.8 cm]). A sturdy side ledge allows gardeners to sit while tending their blooms.

during the winter to prevent damage, so consider something less fragile if you live in a climate with frigid winters. If you select wood, the container walls should be at least 2 inches (5 cm) thick for support; soil is heavy.

Sensor water containers have a reservoir that releases moisture as required; it needs be filled only once every four to six weeks. You can select from boxes large enough to hold a tree or small enough to sit on the windowsill. Whatever the size or shape of the container, be certain the potting soil you use to fill it is suited to the particular plant. Your nursery can guide you when it comes to choosing potting soil and tell you whether there's sufficient space for the root system to properly take hold within the container.

Raised containers can create a dramatic impact by adding color and design and make gardening a lot friendlier for your back.

Spending time outdoors is vital for healthy longevity, and gardening is a pleasant form of outdoor exercise.

Enjoying the Outdoors

If you want to get the utmost pleasure from your outdoor space at any time of day, think about creating areas that offer shade as well as sun. Trees provide natural shade, but if your yard has too few, consider a trellis with closely spaced boards. Plant a climbing rose bush beside the trellis, and as the summers come and go, you'll soon be sitting under a bower of magnificent blossoms. You can also choose a level spot for a weather-worthy table with an umbrella in the center so you can eat or work on your laptop outside in shady comfort. The white plastic version of these tables can cause glare, but if you cover it with a pretty tablecloth, your eyes will thank you.

Outdoor Seating

Comfortable outdoor seating allows you and your guests to fully enjoy the garden. There are basically four different construction materials used for

Quick Fixes

Mark those paths!

By all means, light outdoor paths and walkways for night-time use. But don't forget that those who experience some degree of vision loss can also have difficulties during the day. So highlight pathway edges with landscaping, including brightly colored flowers that create a strong visual contrast.

Ground lights can be used as accent lighting—not only on pathways, but throughout the grounds, including decks and patios.

Swinging in an outdoor bench on a beautiful summer day is one of life's greatest pleasures. For those with balance problems, have someone steady the bench when getting in and out.

garden furniture: wood, wrought iron, plastic, and lightweight aluminum. Although the type you choose is often a matter of personal preference, be attentive to how well your selection supports the universal design principles of safety and access.

• Wood and wrought iron are generally the most attractive choices. You can make them more comfortable by adding well-padded cushioning. Both materials are relatively heavy and not easy to move, but they're stable due to the weight and won't blow about on a windy day.

• Aluminum and plastic are generally the lightest choices and therefore the most portable. Relatively inexpensive, these materials are mostly impervious to the elements. But they can also be flimsy. Choose furniture that is sturdy enough to support your weight. If anyone in your family has mobility problems and often leans on stable objects for balance, lightweight furniture is a poor choice because it tips over easily.

Privacy & Sound Control

Part of the enjoyment of a garde n comes from the quiet, privacy, and peace it can give. If your garden could use a bit of soundproofing, here are a few things you can do to reduce background noise.

• Use lattice walls, vine-covered wire fencing, or ordinary wood fencing. You don't want to add privacy at the cost of ventilation, though, so use open fencing if you live in a climate where breezes are an important source of relief from hot, muggy air.

• Add a bubbling garden fountain. From a simple terra-cotta pot to a tiered fountain, bubbling water sounds can soothe the spirits and help cancel out unwanted sounds.

• Add a berm. This is a raised mound of earth, generally 3 feet (91.5 cm) high at its maximum point, with gently sloping sides. You can form one wherever necessary to block and absorb street noise.

IT'S WISE TO BE SAFE

Grounds & Pathway Lighting

Solar lights use the power of the sun to light walkways and grounds. Check with your local supplier to see if these eco-friendly lights are effective for your area.

Well-lit grounds and pathways are essential for wellness and safety. Good lighting increases the overall beauty of your home and grounds, protects you from intruders, and can minimize the chances of slipping or tripping. Depending on the size of your property, you may need combinations of solar lights, low-voltage lighting, energy-efficient lampposts, and motion-activated lights.

Solar lights or low-voltage ground lights can light the walkway to the front entrance. Solar lights don't require any wiring and are therefore simple to install, but a climate with constant cloud cover or limited sun will limit their effectiveness. A local home-center can advise you on the suitability of solar lights in your particular location. Keep in mind, though, that many solar lights produce only enough light to delineate the edges of the walkway, with minimal spill light on the walkway itself. Low-voltage (12 V) lights offer more illumination than solar lights, use far less electricity than conventional 120 V systems, and you can connect them to a timer that will switch the lights on in the evening and off in the morning.

Illuminating the pathway at nighttime adds safety, security, and—with the right lighting—drama and beauty. Depending on the size of your property, look into a combination of low pathway lights and lampposts.

Longevity Essentials

Nature's Soothing Influence

If a member of your household has Alzheimer's or some other form of dementia, encourage him or her to go outdoors. A little exercise in the fresh air during the day can be calming and therapeutic, as can sitting in a comfortable chair listening to the birds and looking at flowers. But you might want to put up a high, secure (that is, not climbable) fence so the person does not wander off and get lost. Also, fence off all ponds or pools, no matter how shallow. Another important step: check with a local nursery to verify that there are no plants growing in the garden that might be poisonous if ingested.

Gardening with Universal Design in Mind

Why, you might be asking, is gardening being discussed in this book? We know that many people 50+ are passionate about digging in the dirt, and I include myself among them, but we may not have the time or physical abilities to garden like we did years ago. The good news is that you can enjoy gardening at any age, as long as you eliminate the backbreaking-labor component.

Many companies have redesigned garden tools with longer handles so that less bending and reaching are

This inviting garden offers wider walkways (60 inches or 1.5 m) that allow everyone to move easily, including couples strolling side by side, mothers with children in tow, and anyone using a scooter or other type of mobility aid.

necessary; many smaller tools now feature handles that are easier to hold. Choose perennials for years of beauty with minimal care. Low maintenance, thinking green, and cool gadgets are all part of universal design, too, when the benefit is living the life we love.

easy to go green
Reduce Watering

Rather than spending hours standing in your garden with a hose, or wasting water with a sprinkler system that lets only 50 percent of the water reach the plants while the other half is lost to evaporation, select a drip irrigation system. Lay the tube with tiny pinholes along the ground, concealed under mulch or shrubs. When you hook the drip system up to your faucet and turn it on, the water slowly seeps directly into the root system where it's most useful. You can connect any drip system to an electronic water timer that automatically waters the garden on a seven-day schedule up to four times a day.

If you have areas that can't be reached with a drip system, or places you choose to water manually, buy a lightweight hose of rubber and vinyl. These hoses are 50 percent lighter than standard hoses, and infinitely easier to drag around.

Ergonomic gardening tools include cushioned handles for a more comfortable grip and an easy-on-the-knees cushioned pad. The extended handles help when kneeling and standing.

Quick Fixes

Thinking Low Maintenance

When planning your garden, let "low maintenance" be your mantra, and keep this list of indisputable facts nailed to your garden shed:

• A high-maintenance lawn is *not* the only attractive ground cover. Ground covers include perennials, herbs, shrubs, sprawling vines, mosses, and low-growing plants such as ivy and daisies. These plants are not only low- or no-maintenance, but they also provide much more textural variation than a flat expanse of lawn. Why worry about having to cut the grass each week (and maintain the mower) when you could sit on your porch looking out over a field of periwinkle?

• Choose from among the many perennials that reseed themselves year after year. There are so many plants to choose from in most climates that once you've planted a perennial garden, it should offer years of beauty with very little care, assuming that low-maintenance systems are in place to provide ongoing care.

• Automatic and/or sensor watering systems will free you forever from a rigid watering schedule. (See Easy to Go Green on this page.)

• Raised beds and container gardens are easy to get at. Plus, small containers are portable. As the seasons change, you can move them to an area that gets the best conditions, thereby extending the growing season.

• Mulch, mulch, mulch.

Gallery

This inviting patio has lovely plantings and a place for casual dining. The wrought iron table and chairs, with comfortable cushions and a sun umbrella for weather protection, enhances healthy outdoor living.

If you have only one or two short steps, you may be able to create an accessible entrance that will serve you well in the future even if you are fully mobile now. Take a good look at your home and see if you can create a no-step entrance by gently sloping the walkway or adding a ramp with integrated landscaping on the front, side, or back of the house.

Whether your garden is grand and stately or small and charming, provide seating areas that offer shade as well as sun.

CHAPTER 5

Revitalize Your Living Spaces

ALTHOUGH THE FOUNTAIN OF YOUTH remains undiscovered, research shows that happiness is linked to lifestyle choices. Gray is the new Gold—*if* you tap into key activities that keep you in your prime. The choice is yours; like financial health, physical well-being and happiness don't just happen on their own—they take planning and commitment. Adapting your home to make space for healthy aging is an important step in this process.

Recent research indicates that five key factors can promote healthier, happier longevity: *lower stress, strong friendships, lifelong learning, physical activity, and good nutrition.* These longevity essentials seem to thrive in a home environment that enhances relaxation, play, friendly socializing, some brainwork, and moderate but regular exercise. If you refurbish and remodel your home to include true "living" spaces, it's highly likely that healthy longevity won't remain just a nice idea.

Throughout this chapter, I'll share with you research that highlights the keys to healthy and happy aging. I'll suggest ways you can create calm oases for de-stressing, dream up great spaces for socializing, carve out a computer center for working and learning, and design exercise spaces you'll actually want to use—all using universal principles. By combining universal design with wellness, living the second half of your life never looked so good—and maybe it will be even better than the first half!

Living in All Your Rooms

If you are like most people, you have spaces in your home just waiting to be rediscovered, redecorated, and reclaimed for all the things you want to do in the second half of your life. Perhaps you want to entertain more, but this time around in a casual style. Or maybe you have vowed to exercise every day—even in bad weather.

Take a good look at your rooms where there isn't much "living" going on. For example, if you rarely use your living room, jot down all the reasons why. It may be that the seating is uncomfortable and the space feels confined. What if you painted the room a fun color, bought a couple of new chairs with comfy cushions, splurged on a streamlined flat-screen TV, and added a simple card table? Now you could put the "living" back in the living room—and have a casual meal with friends while watching an old movie together or playing a stimulating game of bridge.

If young children have been a little hard on the family room, perhaps it could do double duty as your exercise space if you spruced it up with sturdy, attractive slipcovers, boosted the lighting with a torchiere lamp, and added wicker storage containers that house toys and your exercise gizmos. Now you have a room that's great for your kids and for you.

This gracious living room has many healthy-aging features, including a tall coffee table and a beautiful *painted* floor cloth instead of an area rug to reduce tripping. This room was featured in the first-ever universal design show house in Atlanta, Georgia.

Spaces for Relaxing & Entertaining

It takes thoughtful planning to create a relaxed ambience complete with an open floorplan, a pleasing color palette, and user-friendly furnishings. If you haven't updated your home in a while, redecorating and remodeling can bring new vitality into it and your life.

At certain times in our lives, it may feel like a burden to freshen up our home, but the benefits are truly worth it. What follows are practical suggestions for creating attractive, easy-to-access, and uplifting spaces with just the right furnishings, so you can enjoy your home and be with family and friends, the universal way.

Sitting by the fireplace offers a chance to de-stress, have intimate conversations with loved ones, or curl up solo with a good book or a Sudoku puzzle. The cream-colored walls and tall windows keep the space light and airy. A raised hearth would make the space even better.

Longevity Essentials

Stay Connected

Harvard Medical School has been a leader in exploring the role of social connections in health and life satisfaction. One study with more than 116,000 participants showed that people who had strong relationships had less mental decline, lived more active lives, had fewer physical limitations, and embraced life's difficulties with a more positive attitude than people who were isolated. International research also supports the finding that maintaining social connections is vital to healthy longevity.

Here are some simple tips for staying connected:

• Try something new. Host a weekly book club or start a crafting group.

• Get involved in a volunteer cause. For example, you could start a pedestrian safety audit in your neighborhood or organize a dinner delivery for a friend in need. For many more ideas, visit AARP's site createthegood.org.

• Get connected to the Web; set up a computer station and e-mail your children, grandchildren, and friends. Join an online interest group.

• Throw a potluck dinner and have everyone bring a favorite family recipe.

• Sign up for a free service that allows video "chat" or video calls from your computer, and you can "visit" with relatives who live far away. Each user needs an inexpensive webcam. New laptop computers have built-in webcams. Choose an "instant messenger" service with a company such as Yahoo or MSN, and it will help you get set up.

Take a Seat!

There's nothing quite like curling up in a cozy chair with a good book, or sitting on a comfortable sofa while visiting with friends.

That's why it's important to assess your existing seating to see what may need replacing or updating. Quite often, what was a good fit when you were younger is no longer optimal.

This stylish chair offers a relaxing yet firm seat, and the opening underneath makes it easy to stand up.

You may also find that those older sofas and chairs are now too deep and low, making them uncomfortable and hard to get out of. (The rule of thumb: if your knees are above your hips when seated, it will be extra hard to stand up.)

Whether you prefer a plush sofa with pillows or a lounge chair that reclines, the universal home has seating that is attractive and stylish, and also provides support for your lower back and helps you sit "tall." Explore some of the new furniture designed with ergonomic seating. If you or a guest has "back issues," it's good to offer one chair that you know will always provide comfort and support.

Ergonomic Guidelines

If you're thinking about replacing your existing seating, the following design features offer ergonomic support:

• A seat height of 18 inches (46 cm) and a depth ranging from 19 to 23 inches (48 to 58.5 cm). As an alternative you can use back pillows for seats with greater depth; if a chair is too deep, it's hard both to sit in it and to rise from it.

• Arms that facilitate easy transfers. You'll want the side arms at a height of about 25 inches (63.5 cm) to extend to the front of the seat for support when rising. If they're much higher, you can't use the arms to push off from when rising.

• Look for a back that has a slight incline for relaxation; you'll also want a high back for shoulder, neck, and head support (especially for people who need extra support, including those with Parkinson's disease).

• A "tube" or roll pillow for good lumbar support.

• An open space beneath the chair that allows you to tuck your feet underneath you when rising, giving you greater leverage.

Seat Cushions

Over time, seat cushions "bottom out" and lose their plumpness and support. Soft cushions do not allow proper alignment of the spine: the hips become rotated, causing discomfort. Soft cushions also do not offer a stable transfer surface—you sink further into the cushion when trying to rise. If your cushions need replacing, find a local upholsterer to do the job. Consider an inner wedge of medium-density foam, wrapped with polyester fill, or, for a touch of luxury, down feathers. Be careful though about "firm" foam cushioning—it can be rock hard and quite uncomfortable. If the chair is very old, you may need to have the springs retied or new webbing installed.

Make your seating more user friendly. You can add a few inches to low seating by placing an extra cushion on the chair seat or riser blocks under the sofa legs.

Reclining Chairs

Reclining chairs have always been popular—and for good reason. Just sitting in a recliner with your feet propped up can immediately transport you into the relaxation zone. And they're especially good if you have lower-back problems or need to elevate your feet. Today's recliners offer something for everyone, including modern designs and luxury options such as massage and heat, which can be ideal if you sometimes feel cold. Some newer models, including zero-gravity chairs, elevate the legs above your heart level, known medically as the Trendelenburg position, which is especially good for anyone with a heart condition. These chairs, however, can be hard to get up from unless you purchase one with an electric lift (see Lift-Up Chairs below).

Reclining chairs offer a great seat to unwind and relax. They come in many styles and with a wide array of options, including massage and heat to ease aching muscles and a push-button lift for those who need an extra boost.

IT'S WISE TO BE SAFE

Lift-Up Chairs

Motorized, lift-up chairs can be very helpful—but only resort to them when transferring becomes too difficult. Even getting in and out of a chair can help exercise our muscles. If a loved one has dementia, keep in mind that the controls on motorized chairs often are too complex for the person to manipulate independently. Only use a lift-up chair when a caregiver is present; the person could fall if he or she tries to get up without aid.

For long-term help getting up from a seat, use a cushioned chair with a built-in automatic lift. For temporary help, try a booster cushion like this one placed on top of a favorite chair's existing cushion.

Let's Talk

You can even practice universal design principles in the way you place your furniture. To encourage conversation, arrange the seating so the sofas and chairs are at right angles or parallel to each other but not too far apart. This grouping lets everyone join in, especially those with hearing or vision limitations. For large get-togethers, you may want to create several types of arrangements to allow for both group and one-on-one chats.

The universal living room has a variety of comfortable seating options. This room, for example, has a sofa and three side chairs. All chairs have arms that extend to the front edge, and two have openings under the front that make it easier to stand up.

Tables & Bookcases

Abundant table surfaces, bookcases, and cabinet storage give you plenty of space to showcase your keepsakes, family photos, books, and collectibles. This is important because it helps keep items off the floor, creating the safe, easy movement that's so important in the universal home. Extra tables also provide serving surfaces, very handy when giving a party or potluck dinner. Here we'll look at some creative ways to add multifunctional table and storage space for everyday living, including the new longevity essentials.

Coffee Table

Most people place a coffee table in front of the sofa with side chairs flanking it. Traditionally, the height of a coffee table is 12 to 14 inches (30.5 to 35.5 cm), but a higher table, roughly 24 to 30 inches (61 to 76 cm), is easier to reach and reduces the need to bend. Depending on the placement of the TV, a higher table could interfere with viewing, but a coffee table that's of medium height will be more comfortable for eating or enjoying a cup of tea with a neighbor. If you or a loved one has low vision, make sure the color of the table contrasts with the floor; glass tables are generally not ideal because they are hard to see and easy to trip over. In very small rooms, you can forgo the coffee table altogether and use small, fold-up trays or stackable tables. Just make sure they're not in the way so that no one trips over them.

End Tables

If you have the space, choose large end tables or multipurpose ones to expand your storage, work, and entertaining options.

Here are some possibilities to consider: A large, round, skirted table with a colorful fabric makes a great statement while serving as an extra dining surface for dinner or holiday parties. If you need bonus storage space, choose a wooden chest of drawers, stained or painted to match your décor. This is a great place to store longevity essentials, including brain games, a set of hand weights (for use

A taller sofa table doubles as an extra surface for an afternoon snack or for a sit-down meal during large family get-togethers. The table covering's fresh green color contrasts with the floor, making it easy to see for those with low vision.

while watching TV), and easy-to-grab linens and place mats for an informal or holiday meal. Finally, a small, 40-inch (101.5 cm) or so wrought-iron bookcase adds visual interest—and provides space for a book collection.

"Brain Games" Table

The evidence is in—brain games, including word games of all kinds (for example, crossword puzzles or Sudoku), help maintain and sharpen memory and other cognitive skills. It's nice to have a square or round table in the corner of the room ready for these activities. Make sure you have good direct lighting over the table—or use a table or floor lamp.

Bookcases

These can be freestanding units or combined with a TV, desk, sleep sofa, or even a Murphy bed for overnight guests. Consider bookcases with doors and bottom cabinets for bonus storage space.

Behind the sofa, this handy side table doesn't get in the way, and it provides ample space for a clock, keepsakes, family portraits, and a reading lamp.

easy to go green
Reuse Furniture

If you like the thrill of the hunt, try a second-hand store for furniture. Not only can you find substantial savings, but you'll also be recycling used furniture. In addition, many older pieces (before the 1950s) and antiques weren't made with harmful chemicals. An environment-friendly fresh coat of paint may be all that's needed to spruce up your second-hand purchase and go green.

If you're looking for salvaged goods, try a reuse store, the new green home-improvement store. They carry items ranging from old doors with peeling paint to gorgeous vintage fireplace mantels. There are 1,000 reuse stores throughout the country, with Habitat for Humanity running more than half of them. Check out Habitat's ReStores to find a national directory of store locations.

If your living space needs freshening up, go green and buy furniture from a thrift store or a reuse store. You can find treasures at bargain prices.

Entertainment Centers

Television not only connects us to the global community, but it can entertain, educate, and take us to remote and exotic environments, all from the comfort of our own home. When used intentionally and with discipline, TV can help us maintain a healthy brain by engaging us in lifelong learning and keeping us informed about local and world events.

Where to Place It?

Streamlined flat-screen TVs are so attractive, they can be "displayed" on a low console table for easy viewing, housed in a large entertainment center, or mounted on a wall. Although flat-screen TVs are shown in ads and in stores mounted high up, this location can cause neck strain. It's better to situate the TV so your eyes are level with the middle of the screen when you're seated. Depending on your

When choosing an entertainment center, look for one that places the TV at an ergonomic viewing height so your eyes are level with the middle of the screen when watching a program. This TV is placed a bit higher than specialists recommend, but as long as you are not a couch potato, it may be comfortable enough for you.

room layout, you can place your sofa directly facing the TV with chairs at the side, or place rows of lounge chairs in front of a home-theater screen.

Television Size

The size of your TV will depend on the size of your room, the viewing distance, the type of TV, and your budget. For the main TV, a larger screen (such as 36 to 48 inches [91.5 to 122 cm]) is ideal if your home is a gathering spot for family get-togethers, and watching sports or movies is an integral part of that tradition. Or you may simply enjoy the impact and immediacy of a larger screen, especially when watching travel or nature shows. If you have a visual impairment, a larger screen can help you better enjoy the image. Be sure to check with the manufacturer to see if you have the recommended viewing distance, as it varies depending on the viewing angles and type of television (flat panel, plasma, or projection).

Quick Fixes

User-Friendly TV

Use a remote control that has large numbers and buttons that light up. It's much easier to use if you're having difficulty with either hand movements or vision.

What should you do if you're experiencing more hearing loss than your partner or housemate? Display the text by using the "captions" function on your TV when it's available. Although not always provided by all channels, most TVs manufactured since 1993 can show captions. So if you have an older TV, it's time to update. Or consider using a headset that increases volume for you without raising the volume for the whole room.

Longevity Essentials

Brain Workouts

Brain health is vital to healthy longevity. According to Dr. Paul Nussbaum, neurologist, researcher, and author of *Your Brain Health Lifestyle* (Word Association, 2009), five key factors support brain health: social connections, physical activity, spirituality (for example, meditation or religious services), nutrition, and mental stimulation.

Research shows that mental stimulation, keeping your brain active and challenged, has a positive effect on brain health. A National Institutes of Health study of cognitive training in healthy adults—the largest such study ever conducted—found improvements in memory, concentration, and problem-solving skills. Participants who had mild memory impairment were also able to improve their reasoning skills and become faster at processing visual information.

Here are some fun brain workouts you can do at home:

• Play computer-based brain games.

• Take an online class and learn something new and exciting.

• Start a new business from home.

• Play puzzle and board games.

Brain workouts, including cards and crossword puzzles, can help sharpen memory and keep your brain healthy and fit.

Lighting for Healthy Living

We all know that lighting is a key design element—it can create a room's look and feel. But did you know that in universal design terms, lighting can also promote healthy longevity? Simply put, good lighting helps us see and function better. Review the lighting section in chapter 3 on page 40 for information that will help you choose abundant and easily adjustable light. Here are three tips to help you create relaxed, and uplifting lighting schemes.

1. Get the right bulb. For most people, eco-friendly compact fluorescent lightbulbs (CFLs) are an excellent choice for a warm, bright light. But if you have high ceilings and recessed fixtures, low-voltage bulbs may be a more efficient choice, delivering more of a downward punch. For reading or close-up work, check out full-spectrum bulbs; they filter out yellow light rays, making colors crisper and print easier to read.

2. Leave background lighting on when watching TV at night. Lower the lights rather than turn them off,

This living room has abundant natural light from windows and a long wall of sliding glass doors. Sheer drapes can soften harsh glare when needed.

as the strong contrast between the brightness of the screen and the darkness of the room can cause eyestrain and headaches.

3. Let the light shine—on the activity. Any area where you plan to relax, read a book, or engage in a challenging brain game will be more enjoyable with good task lighting. A hanging ceiling lamp, a table lamp, or a reading lamp with a flexible arm gives you light exactly where you want it.

Color

Light-colored walls reflect more light and make small rooms look bigger. But if you've always wanted a room with deep cinnabar walls, now may be the time to live your dreams. Painting the ceiling a crisp white and choosing a light-colored carpet will keep the room from getting too dark and feeling heavy. Since darker-colored rooms require additional lighting, consider using large table lamps with three-way bulbs and a torchiere or two.

When choosing colors for walls, fabrics, and floors, take a look at the warm tones within any color group; as we age, we more vividly perceive warm tones—especially colors comprised of yellows, reds, and oranges. A warm yellow sofa against a pale cream wall, for example, is both charming and functional. Keep in mind that furniture should be in a color that contrasts with the floor and wall to demarcate its edges; this is essential for anyone with low vision.

Contrasting colors make it easier for those with vision loss to navigate. Use this as an excuse to express your personality! For example, this cherry red sofa and the bright apple green walls stand out against the lighter colored flooring and show off an expressive spirit.

This hanging alabaster pendant shines light onto the table and onto the ceiling for a soft, diffuse effect.

Spaces for Computer Stations & Home Offices

Computer stations and home offices have become an integral part of our daily lives. Millions of Americans have designated computer areas at home, with spare bedrooms transformed into "CEO" offices and living room corners into communication centers, smart-home command stations, and even brain fitness centers.

As you know, the computer and Internet have revolutionized the way we live, and have become indispensable tools for healthy longevity. The benefits are seemingly endless: You can communicate with people all over the world, stay in touch with family, tap into reference libraries, take online classes, play brain games, and get local and international news—all without leaving home. And with a smart-home program, you can control your home's lighting, heating, and security—even when you're traveling (see page 57).

If you'd rather stay home and work in your pajamas, join the millions of people telecommuting to work or running their own companies from the comfort of their homes. Retirees are reinventing their lives by starting new businesses for the adventure, the satisfaction that comes from working and contributing to society, and the extra income.

There are many ways to create a great space for a computer center without spending a fortune and without looking corporate. Whether you're a seasoned computer user or a novice about to take the plunge, here are some key ideas for setting up or making your home office or computer center function and look better. (If you're new to computers, check out computertrainingschools.com or seniornet.org for help finding local computer training centers for adults 50+.)

Need a room for a home office but can't find the space? Consider erecting a semiprivate half-wall in a large room to define the area while allowing light and views. Curving the wall creates a soft, dynamic line, and the warm wood floor and fun wall color enliven the space.

Rich colors and ergonomic furnishings make this space a good marriage of style and function. When designing with wellness in mind, though, consider the safety of the person using the space. A chair like this one with casters adds convenience for some, but can be a fall hazard for others.

Identify the Space

Whether it's a separate room or a corner of a room, claim a space you love, and you'll enjoy working there all the more.

A Separate Room

If you're telecommuting, running a home business, or just logging a lot of computer hours per day, a quiet, separate room (a den or a spare bedroom) with lots of space and a nice view is your best bet. Include a sleep sofa and attractive storage containers (for example, canvas or wicker boxes), and the space can easily double as a guest room when needed. An office in the garage can also be a great choice, especially for those who like the feeling of getting up and going out to the office! If this is a viable option, check with your electrician about adding outlets, heating, and air conditioning.

User-friendly design features for this home office include a wide entry, good lighting, and plenty of bookshelves. The sliding doors provide privacy without taking up space, and the extra-wide, no-threshold entryway makes coming and going easy and safe. With the addition of a sleep sofa, this room could also serve as a welcoming guest room for visitors who require first-floor accommodations.

Carving Out Space in an Existing Room

A separate room isn't the only, or even the best, option. Whether the space is large or small, the key is to efficiently use what you have: a small, organized space can function better than a larger one that's disorganized. With a bit of creativity and planning, you can carve out a portion of any room and still keep its original feel.

Take a good look at your living and dining rooms, and even the kitchen. A home office, including your computer, printer, and files, can be concealed in a beautiful armoire along a dining or living room wall, for instance. That way, the work area doesn't take center stage. Or place an attractive desk at a right angle to the sofa, facing into the room. Add a chair, a beautiful lamp, your laptop, and, voilà, you've created an attractive computer center. You can also position your desk in a corner, surrounded by bookshelves with bottom storage cabinets. Make sure to leave plenty of space for people to pass. Finally, if the kitchen is your favorite room in the house, you can use your laptop at a cozy breakfast nook or at a built-in desk.

Get a Good Work Surface

One of the most important features of your office space is your work surface. You'll want a good amount of table surface on which to spread out papers or files and room for a lamp, a telephone, and an in/out box. Whether you choose a freestanding or built-in desk depends on the space, your budget, and your preferences.

The standard desktop height—29½ inches (75 cm)—may be an ideal height for most people for writing, but not for typing on a keyboard. When you use your keyboard, your forearms should be flat, from your elbows to your wrists, and roughly parallel to the floor. Think about installing a slide-out keyboard tray so that your keyboard is at a comfortable height. This will also help you avoid carpal tunnel syndrome and other wrist problems.

Control the Lighting

The room's lighting should be more or less equivalent to the brightness of the computer monitor; a sharp contrast between the two can cause eyestrain and headaches. Background lighting can come from different sources, including daylight and floor lamps. Choose window coverings that allow you to control the light, because glare on the monitor makes it difficult to use. Consider an adjustable desk lamp on either side of the screen to illuminate reading materials and the desktop. If you do a lot of writing, place the lamp on the side that's opposite your dominant hand to avoid casting a shadow on the paper.

This colorful office, hidden behind retractable doors, has ample task lighting, storage shelves, and a fun purple work surface. For extended sitting, you'll want an office chair with good back support and a cushioned seat.

If you enjoy your kitchen space, think about converting a corner into a place to pay bills, plan menus, and keep up with e-mail. Here, under-cabinet lighting illuminates the work surface, and side drawers keep clutter to a minimum.

Invest in an Ergonomic Chair

If you'll be sitting for several hours a day, take your time finding a desk chair that's a good ergonomic fit for you and the type of work you'll be doing. Whether you're involved in computer work or reading paper documents, sitting in a poorly designed chair can lead to back problems. And if the chair isn't comfortable, you won't enjoy working in your home office.

When selecting a new chair, choose one that supports a variety of seated positions. In other words, look for a chair that allows you to make lots of adjustments.

• Adjusting the seat height ensures that your feet remain flat on the floor, with your thighs parallel to the floor. If your current chair is too high (and not adjustable), use a footrest to avoid circulation problems.

• Adjusting the seat's depth ensures that your legs and back are properly supported. For healthy circulation, the undersides of your knees should not be pressed against the front edge of the seat; you should be able to sit far enough back in the chair to get good lumbar support.

• Adjusting the seat pan (that's what you sit on) gives you flexibility for sitting in a semi-reclined position for reading or in a forward position for desk work.

• Adjusting the backrest for good lumbar support is crucial to healthy posture. If your current chair does not provide this, try adding a back pillow.

• Adjustable armrests, both for width and height, give you the option of using the armrests when reading or using the phone, or moving them out of the way when typing. (Experts say you should not rest your arms or wrists

A good office chair provides lumbar support and even weight distribution. A good chair offers a number of adjustable features such as arm height and seat tilt. If you spend a lot of time sitting, consider a pressure-relieving surface like memory foam or a breathable mesh-like membrane for a more comfortable seat.

while typing.) Using armrests during non-typing activities—for example, reading news on the Internet—can ease neck and shoulder tension.

In addition, look for a rounded ("waterfall") edge at the front of the seat that prevents pressure on your legs and knees. A five-legged base adds stability. Finally, it's best if casters suit the room's flooring: hard casters for carpeting and rubber-coated ones for hard surfaces. Otherwise, the chair can easily slide out from under

you when you stand up or sit down, causing a fall. If you have serious balance problems, choose a chair without casters. These features and design details are even more important if more than one person will be using the chair.

This fresh and inviting work space, tucked away in a small corner room, is well illuminated. Light colors on the floor and walls make the space look bigger than it actually is.

Provide for Storage

An organized work area is a must for keeping piles of paper and "stuff" off your desk, especially if it's in a main living area. Think of all the storage space you need for your home office or computer station, including space for printer paper, computer program manuals, reference books, and files. If storage space is limited near your desk, find space in a nearby room for items you use less frequently.

When it comes to storage, look around and be creative. You can use wall shelves, a wall storage unit, a nearby closet, or file cabinets, but don't forget to consider rattan baskets, fabric boxes, or an armoire.

Plan for Outlets

Plan for all the electrical outlets you'll need. Have a telephone jack installed or use a cell phone if you have reliable service. In some areas, you'll also have the choice of an Internet phone, which can be less expensive. Include power-surge protectors to guard your computer and data. If you need new outlets, mount them 18 to 24 inches (46 to 61 cm) above the floor for easy access.

Personalize Your Space

And now for the fun part. Just because it's a home office or computer station doesn't mean it has to look like an office. It's your work space—and at this stage of the game, you can decorate it any way you want! Add a fresh, lively color or a sedate, calming one to set the tone you want. Add the warmth of wood or personal touches to make the space inviting and uplifting. Hang up favorite photographs or other artwork, even if you have to move in pictures from another room, to make this space one that you'll truly enjoy.

Spaces for Exercise

Many of the diseases once thought to be a normal part of aging are now attributed to a lack of exercise. The Centers for Disease Control and Prevention (CDC) tell us that regular exercise reduces the risk of mobility problems while contributing to healthy bones, muscles, and joints. And that's not all. The CDC also reports that exercise can decrease the need for hospitalizations, physician visits, and medications. If it's beginning to sound a bit like a magic pill, well, it is. It's also been shown that exercise reduces symptoms of anxiety and depression and even slows cognitive decline.

With such health rewards, fitness specialists have created exercise programs for just about anyone, including those who need to sit, stand, or recline. You'll be relieved to know that physical activity does not need to be strenuous to be beneficial.

Exercise as You Age

The National Institute on Aging tells us that strength and balance exercises help prevent falls as we get older—and help keep our bones strong and healthy. Much of the loss of muscle and balance experienced during aging is preventable if you keep using those muscles and practicing your balance.

And the good news is—it's never too late to start. Research by Dr. Maria Fiatarone at the Hebrew Rehabilitation Center in Boston showed that even older nursing-home residents increased their muscle strength, walking speed, and stair-climbing power after a 10-week exercise program. There are many things you can do outside your home to keep fit—join a club, go swimming, or take brisk walks in nearby parks or in shopping malls on cold days.

Exercise goes hand in hand with healthy longevity, so choose a room that you love to be in and you'll enjoy your workout so much more. In this room, you can catch up on the day's events or watch a DVD of a beautiful outdoor setting on the large flat-screen TV.

Here are some ways to make exercise a part of your everyday life.

• Create a "fitness center" in a space you love to be in.

• Do something you enjoy that raises your heart rate—consider a back-friendly recumbent bike or a treadmill.

• Make your stairs exercise-friendly. Install handrails on both sides, replace worn-out carpeting or treads, remove any loose area carpets at the landings, and be sure to have plenty of good lighting. You now have a built-in daily exercise program.

• Try yoga or Tai Chi. If your balance isn't what it used to be, install a handrail to hold on to while doing exercises.

• Rake or garden.

If you're new to exercise, remember to start slowly and gradually work your way up to more vigorous exercise. If you're 65 or older or you already have a medical condition, talk to your healthcare provider before starting something new.

Setting Up an Exercise Space

It's not always easy to exercise, especially if you're not used to working out and your joints or muscles are stiff from inactivity. But even individuals with limited movement due to a condition such as Parkinson's disease experience beneficial results from exercise. Experts say that the key to starting—and staying—with an exercise program is finding an activity that you really enjoy. Then once you begin

to feel the benefits—increased energy, a better night's sleep, stronger muscles, more supple joints, and a sharper mind—it's hard not to exercise.

Here are two considerations when setting up an exercise area at home (or making the one you have even better).

Keep It Light

If you're a morning person who has recently discovered the benefits of exercise, but you don't know where to put the treadmill, I suggest choosing a location that you really love. You'll log more miles if you place the equipment in a sunny room that's easy to get to instead of the basement. If you have a guest room, it can do double duty as an exercise room—and your guests can also enjoy a good workout.

Outdoor Lover

Perhaps you love the outdoors but find you're going out less and less in bad weather and aren't getting the exercise you used to. You want to start an exercise program at home, but you're not sure what to do.

You'll probably enjoy exercising at home more if you place your equipment in a room with a view of the outdoors, like a closed-in patio or a guest room that overlooks a garden. If you don't have the space or the view, just bring the outdoors into your home. For example, place your bicycle machine in front of a TV or computer monitor, and have a great virtual outdoor bike ride: specially created DVDs can take you on tours of beautiful natural settings, including the vineyards of California, the beaches of the Caribbean, or the lavender fields in the South of France.

Gallery

Lighting promotes healthy longevity. Well-illuminated rooms can help you see and function better, enhance your mood, and keep you from falling. This room has plenty of overhead lighting and a large expanse of windows for natural light; the addition of table lamps would help illuminate the "mid zone," especially important for a room with dark furniture.

Everyone—including young or old wheelchair users and families with strollers—can benefit from a universal design home. If your living and dining areas are confined, consider removing a wall to create more free-flowing spaces. This combined kitchen-dining room has open places, no-threshold entryways, and several spots where you can enjoy a meal or snack.

THE IDEAL BEDROOM IS A TRANQUIL, quiet place, a sanctuary free from stress, the place where you renew your strength and prepare to face the joys and challenges of a new day. Its essential purpose, of course, is enabling the kind of sleep that allows us to live our lives fully; even a little sleep deprivation can have serious consequences.

You also may read, meditate, and exercise in the universal bedroom. And you'll certainly want a streamlined closet to ensure that you can access your clothes and shoes easily.

As you age, you may want your bedroom to become a healing place. With today's advanced technologies, you or a loved one can receive many medical therapies in the comfort and privacy of your own bedroom.

In this chapter, I'll show you how to create a bedroom where you can live, sleep, or dream. Whether you're updating furnishings or remodeling the entire room, your main goals are to make sure your room is accessible, organized, and filled with optimal lighting, comfortable seating, and a mattress that fits your needs.

Easy Come, Easy Go

One of the biggest issues that emerge as we age is where to locate the bedroom. Begin by asking yourself if your current bedroom is ready to accommodate your needs well into your 90s or even beyond. Could you heal and recuperate there after a hospital stay? If a parent were to come live with you, is there a bedroom that could safely and conveniently meet his or her needs?

First-Floor Bedroom

A first-floor bedroom (and bathroom) has the huge advantage of not having a flight of stairs leading to it. Even if you have no problem bounding up and down the stairs right now, there's a good chance that at some point in your life, it'll become more challenging. If your first floor is too small to accommodate a bedroom, consider enlarging a den, converting a porch, or building an addition, depending on your home's structure, your budget, and your preferences. Add sliding glass doors without a threshold, or with a low one, and your bedroom now has easy access to the outdoors. But if you're in a pinch and a close friend or relative is coming for a short stay, you can use a sleep sofa, a daybed, or a Murphy bed in a first-floor room.

A first-floor bedroom gives you more options to live at home or to offer welcoming accommodation for family and friends. When choosing a bed, however, be careful of the height; this extra high bed is better suited for a tall person.

Second-Floor Bedroom

If moving to the first floor is not an option, give some thought to what you would do if you could no longer climb stairs. If you have a healthy budget, an in-home elevator is an attractive and convenient solution. A wheelchair lift or stair lift can also be helpful, depending on your situation (see Home Elevators in chapter 3 on page 52). For example, my Aunt Blanche, knowing that she had only six months to live, rented a stair lift and, with her family's support, had it installed. This gave her the freedom to enjoy the simple pleasures that we tend to take for granted, such as having a meal with friends and family outside the confines of the bedroom—in the shared social spaces of her dining room and kitchen.

A main feature of a universal design home is accessibility, increasing your chances of remaining in your home for a lifetime. This spacious light-filled bedroom has a no-step doorway leading to an outdoor garden.

Get Wired (in a Good Way)

The bedroom is not only a refuge, but increasingly it's becoming a communication center. With the right wiring and gizmos, we can control our environment and communicate with others for improved safety, health, and well-being.

For Health & Wellness

With the coming shift of health care from expensive hospital settings to the home, getting wired (for computers, sensors, and various home health products) will allow you to prevent, monitor, and treat medical conditions without having to leave the comfort of home. For instance, you can install the latest cable or wireless systems, along with multiple outlets, on each side of the bed, so you'll have more options when it comes to receiving treatments in your own home instead of in a crowded residence.

Environmental Controls

Consider all the possible bedside controls that could make your life easier and more empowering. What might seem like a luxury now may be essential for living independently, especially if you live alone and have a mobility limitation.

If you're planning to upgrade your electrical wiring, explore the various bedside controls that are available; there are controls for lighting, temperature, window treatments, music, security—there's even a remote video door-answering system. You can purchase stand-alone systems for individual controls or packages for the whole home. With an individual lighting control, you can turn off the bedroom and hallway lights without getting out of bed. With a whole home automation system, on the other hand, house lights gently fade (including the bedroom's), blinds shut tight, the security system arms, indoor temperatures adjust, and doors lock. And the next morning, you can awaken to the welcoming aroma of freshly brewed coffee and your favorite symphony playing on the stereo!

If you're recuperating from surgery and expecting a visitor, a stand-alone system lets you see who's at the door on video and buzz them in. Also, don't forget the importance of simple everyday technologies for nighttime emergencies: as cell phone service is not always reliable, and the keypad can be hard to see without glasses, you'll want a landline phone with large, easy-to-read buttons that light up in the dark. If your situation warrants it, also consider a personal emergency response system.

IT'S WISE TO BE SAFE

Louder Is Better

Install smoke detectors that sound a high-decibel, extra-loud alarm and flash a strobe light, but be warned: some of these alarms are extremely loud for those without hearing impairments.

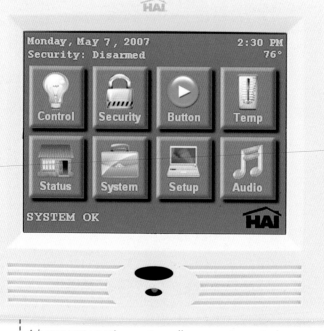

A home automation system allows you to control your environment with a simple push of a button: lights, small appliances, security, and temperature settings. Choose a large LCD panel with text and icons in bright colors.

Boost the Lighting

Abundant natural and interior light that's easily adjustable will keep you safer, happier, and functioning at your best.

The bedroom is one of the most important rooms to make eco-friendly because you spend so much time there. Avoiding harsh chemicals in interior products and finishes is important to everyone's health, but especially if you have asthma or allergies.

Natural Light & Window Coverings

A combination of window treatments usually gives optimal light control. To soften incoming light, use sheer curtains, blinds, or shades. To control the direction and amount of incoming light, especially bright sunlight, choose blinds. Drapes offer good privacy while adding a splash of color, texture, and acoustical control.

This spacious bedroom has plenty of floor space and abundant natural and indoor light. Ceiling fans can cool a house a few degrees by themselves and can augment air conditioning.

These eco-friendly woven shades help control outdoor light while providing a bright color accent. For a master bedroom, consider using blinds along with shades for superior light control during the daytime.

Quick Fixes

Choosing a New Paint Color

After a visit to the paint store, bring home several swatches of the colors you're considering and tape them to the wall. Choose two of your favorites and buy a small can of both colors. Paint a 2 x 2-foot (61 x 61 cm) sample of each, and view the colors over the course of several days—in the morning, afternoon, and evening light. Then pick your favorite. If it's not what you were expecting after the first coat (and it often isn't), choose a lighter or darker color for the second coat.

easy to go green
Eco-Makeovers in the Bedroom

Window coverings. Use hemp or woven shades made from grasses, reeds, and bamboo to filter the light, reduce glare, and add a natural tone (but make sure to pair them with draperies for privacy). Another option is blinds made from untreated natural products from sustainable forests, such as bamboo.

Drapery, chair, and bedding fabrics. Choose untreated organic cotton and wool for your window, seating, and bedding needs. And if you think that limits your options, you'll be surprised to know that organic cotton sheets are available in sateen, percale, damask, and flannel—even with lace trim.

Floor coverings. Specify carpeting with no chemical treatments, such as permanent stain resistance, mothproofing, or antimicrobial agents (fungicide). Recycled materials, as well as cottons and wools, are excellent eco-friendly choices, as is keeping the wooden floors bare (which helps prevent dust mites). For more information, see Flooring in chapter 3 on page 53.

Furniture. If you're purchasing new bedside tables and a dresser, look for wood from sustainable forests, as well as nontoxic finishes, such as beeswax and tung oil.

Paint. If you're considering sprucing up your bedroom with new color on the walls, use a low-VOC (volatile organic compound) paint, as it has fewer toxins.

Lighting. Remember to use energy-efficient compact fluorescent lightbulbs (CFLs) and LED night-lights whenever possible.

Plants. Houseplants are the most eco-friendly air purifiers you can buy. Plants absorb toxins (such as formaldehyde) through their roots and leaves, then turn the poisons into nutrients. Before buying them, consider the light, humidity, and temperature of your bedroom to make the best selection. Top air-purifying picks include orchids and broad sword ferns, as well as rubber, spider, and snake plants.

These sheers filter incoming light effectively. To provide total privacy in the bedroom, add another window treatment, such as blinds or full-length drapes.

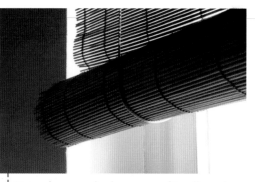

Natural woven shades are eco-friendly and increase the room's comfort by controlling glare and filtering daylight effectively.

Indoor Lighting

A light switch at the entrance to your bedroom can help prevent a fall—turning the light on *before* you enter a room reduces your chances of tripping over a stray shoe or a cat sprawled in the walkway. And every bed needs a good reading lamp next to it or behind it on the wall. To avoid fumbling around and reaching up for light switches (especially if arthritis has reduced your dexterity), install a rocker light switch on the bedside wall or table. Or you can simply insert a touch switch into the lamp socket. You'll also want a good reading lamp placed next to a comfortable chair. A gooseneck lamp with a swinging neck that can shine light directly on the magazine or book is a good option. Finally, ceiling light tends to shine in your eyes when you're in bed; a clever and vision-friendly alternative is a wall valance that illuminates the room with soft indirect lighting.

Universal design lets you choose a modern, traditional, or eclectic look to express your personal aesthetics. If your bedroom has the space, consider creating a comfortable seating area.

This innovative valance bathes the wall with light while illuminating the room with soft indirect lighting.

Spacious Layouts

One of the most important ways to practice universal design in the bedroom is to make sure there's enough space for you or a loved one to easily move around with a walker or wheelchair. You may want to make sure there's room to have a caregiver by your side. A minimum of 3 feet (1 m) of clear space on both sides of the bed and 5 feet (1.5 m) on a third side makes it possible to move around without banging against walls and furniture or having to back out of the room if you're using a scooter.

If your existing bedroom is too small, you could combine it with an adjacent guest room or remove a couple of closets. This may be one of the best investments you can make in terms of remodeling your home for the second half of your life. If this is not feasible, at least make certain the room has a 34-inch (86.5 cm) clear doorway with no or low thresholds; this makes for a roomier, no-hassle entrance. You can also increase the bedroom's usable floor space by installing sliding doors instead of conventional swing-out doors, at both the room's entrance and the closet.

Comfortable Seating

A good, comfortable chair invites you to relax. Whether you're sitting down to read, meditate, or drink a morning cup of tea, you'll want a chair that's not too low or deep, with a supportive seat (not super soft or hard) and side arms. If you or a loved one prefers sitting or napping in a recliner but needs an extra boost when getting up, consider a lift-up chair. (See Lift-Up Chairs in chapter 5 on page 88 for more information.)

If you love reading in bed, an upright bed-reading pillow is a more ergonomic choice than bunching and stacking multiple soft down pillows. Designed to support the back, neck, and shoulders and align the spine properly, bed-reading pillows are available in local bedding and home stores or online.

When reading in bed, use a special back pillow with lumbar support to promote better posture and increase comfort. If you're prone to allergies, select a pillow with hypoallergenic filling and an unbleached cotton shell.

IT'S WISE TO BE SAFE

Flooring

Dense, low-pile carpeting or wood floors with a matte finish are your best choices for flooring in your bedroom. As already noted, thick carpeting, area rugs, and wood floors with slippery finishes are all causes of preventable falls. It's easy to use wheeled devices on low-pile carpeting. (See Wall-to-Wall Carpeting on page 53 and Wood Floors on page 54 for details.)

Wall-to-wall carpeting in the bedroom provides warmth, sound absorption, and soft comfort underfoot. Choose a low-pile carpet to prevent tripping, which is a constant risk with plush carpets. Also, It's harder to wheel over thick carpeting.

A Great Mattress =
A Good Night's Sleep

A quiet, restful night of sleep is restorative at any age—but it's especially important in the second half of your life. Sleep patterns change as we get older; the National Institute on Aging (NIA) tells us that changes in circadian rhythms often interfere with the ability to sleep well. Without enough restful sleep, you're more likely to be irritable, depressed, inattentive, and forgetful. You can also have more accidents, especially falls.

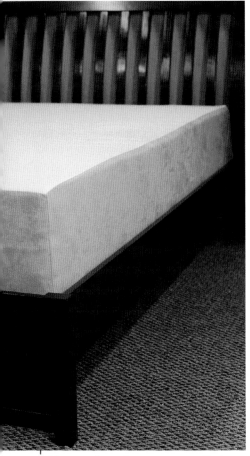

Memory foam has pressure-relieving properties. Mattresses come in various grades and qualities, some with a pillow top for more comfort. People tend to have strong opinions about this mattress type; make sure you test it out in a showroom before purchasing.

Now for the good news: the NIA says we can promote good sleep with a healthy lifestyle and a sleep-friendly environment. Getting enough exercise is one way; so is avoiding rich foods before bedtime and caffeine after 2:00 P.M. Some people find that soothing balms, such as warm baths, soft music, gentle yoga, and meditation, contribute to better sleep. But of the many elements that promote restful z's, the most important of all is surely a comfortable bed.

Shopping for a Mattress

There are many factors besides the mattress that contribute to restorative sleep, including your physical and mental health; but a *bad* mattress can almost *guarantee* a poor night's sleep. Maybe you've even forgotten what it feels like to wake up refreshed. Sleeping on a comfortable, supportive mattress won't cure everyone's insomnia or aching joints and muscles, but if your innerspring mattress is older than 10 or 15 years, it may be a culprit.

If you haven't purchased a mattress in the last decade, you're in for a surprise. Today there's a dizzying array of mattresses; each type comes with its own bells and whistles, from specialty "pillow tops" to zoned layers that provide different degrees of pressure relief.

Unfortunately, it's difficult to find reliable guidelines. Manufacturers change model names for different retailers, making it impossible to compare models from store to store. In addition, significant differences—including quilting, padding, and springs—are hidden from sight *inside* the mattresses. Since these characteristics affect comfort, buying a new mattress can be a challenging task.

Longevity Essentials

Six Good Sleep Tips

1. Sleep on a comfortable, supportive mattress that doesn't sag. If your mattress is older than 10 or 15 years, replace it.

2. Use a supportive pillow that will keep your neck and back properly aligned. If your pillow is flat and worn out, it's time for a new one.

3. If your partner's movements keep you awake at night, sleep in a separate bed or replace your mattress with a "low motion transfer" mattress (see page 115).

4. Minimize outdoor light with blinds, shades, or drapes.

5. Use LED night-lights. Research shows they don't interfere, as incandescent lights can, with the ability to fall back to sleep.

6. Control the room's temperature—if it's too hot or too cold, it can disrupt sleep.

Although *Consumer Reports* gets more questions on mattresses than on any other product except cars, they don't publish mattress ratings due to the absence of consistency in model names. Do your homework: before heading out on your shopping expedition, read about the pros and cons of the various types of mattresses.

Mattress Shopping Etiquette

Make sure you have the time and patience to shop for a new mattress. Wear comfortable clothing and go to the showroom with a book, magazine, or newspaper. Then spend at least 5 to 10 minutes lying on each bed you're interested in. Narrow your choices, and go back the next day and, this time, spend 10 to 15 minutes on each bed in the positions you tend to sleep in. Remember—you're the only one who can tell which type of mattress is good for you.

Don't rely solely on brands, prices, model names, salespersons, or even cost. According to *Consumer Reports*, sometimes there can be a substantial difference in price between two mattresses that are essentially the same.

Most showrooms allow an exchange within a given time period, often 30 days. They invariably charge a fee plus shipping costs, so it's not cheap. Very few sellers allow outright returns, as they're forbidden by law from reselling the mattress. Some retailers who claim to accept returns allow only in-store credit, which is more like an exchange. Finally, keep in mind that it will be difficult to make a claim against a warranty. It's hard to prove that there is anything wrong with the mattress, apart from your not liking it.

Key Mattress Features

The two most important features to consider when buying a mattress are the level of firmness and the type of mattress—innerspring, foam, or air.

Firmness

Contrary to conventional wisdom, a very firm mattress is rarely ideal for older adults because it can exacerbate aching muscles and joints in the shoulders, back, hip, or neck. Don't rely on labels alone, as various manufacturers may characterize firmness and softness differently.

Test the mattress before you buy to find one that's comfortable. What one company labels "firm," another may call "medium." Select a bed at a safe height as well. If you need a footstool to get into bed, the bed is too high!

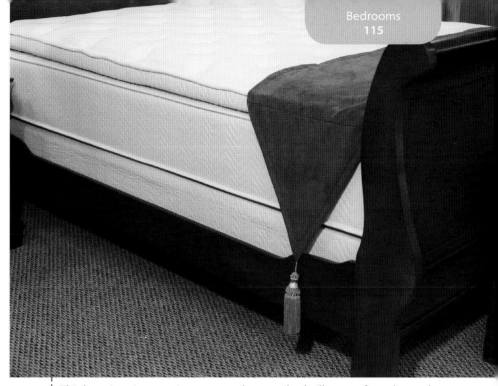

Mattress Types

The three popular mattress types on the market today are innerspring coil, foam (both memory/open-cell foam and latex), and air; some are a combination of these. For example, an innerspring mattress may have a plush pillow top filled with foam or other materials. And most foam mattresses are made with several different types of foams; they're then marketed as the type of foam that predominates.

• **Innerspring.** These coil spring mattresses generally have a life of 10 to 15 years; after that, they lose their ability to support the spine properly, causing discomfort and, possibly, sleepless nights. Innerspring mattresses are available in different "strengths," from soft to very firm. Consider a medium-firm mattress, one that allows your body to relax while keeping your spinal column properly aligned.

• **Foam.** There are many similarities between the two specialty types of foam, memory and latex. They're both open-cell mattresses, which means the cells collapse under pressure and don't push back, thereby reducing pressure at the points where your weight presses the hardest; for instance, shoulders and hips. Think of the open cells in the foam as balloons with "leaks"—when your weight presses down, the air leaks out. This is the opposite of conventional polyurethane foam, in which closed cells retain their pressure and push back against your weight, creating pressure. Both memory and latex foam offer pressure relief, good spinal alignment, and overall support.

There are major differences in the comfort and feel of memory and latex mattresses. *Memory foam* is made out of viscoelastic foam. There are many models to choose from, with various combinations of padding and pillow tops, which can affect the comfort of the mattress. Memory foam mattress-

This luxurious innerspring mattress has a quilted pillow top for enhanced comfort. Regardless of the mattress type, be careful of the mattress's height. To reduce the risk of falling, your feet should touch the floor when you sit on the bed.

es have been used in some health care facilities for their pressure-reducing properties.

But this mattress is not for everyone. It feels very different from a traditional mattress, and people tend either to love it or hate it. One of the main complaints is that turning over can be challenging because you tend to sink into the bed. In addition, some people find this mattress too hot and too hard. It does tend to "sleep hot" because less skin is exposed to the air, which prevents cooling. Also, memory foam is temperature-sensitive; in a cool bedroom, it's relatively firm, but in warm, humid environments it's squishy.

Latex foam also reduces pressure and provides a supportive surface. It can be either all natural (from the rubber tree) or synthetic. Latex mattresses cost more than memory foam, but a main advantage is they aren't temperature-sensitive like memory foam, so they don't "sleep hot" and they remain at the same level of firmness.

The advantages of both memory and latex foam mattresses include not having to turn them over every couple of months, as you do with innerspring

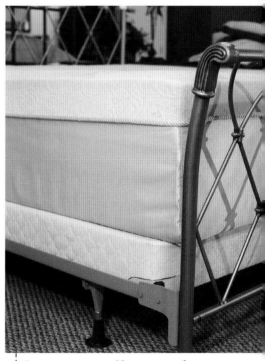

Latex mattresses, like memory foam beds, have pressure-relieving properties, plus a few other advantages, but they're more expensive. When choosing new bedding, think comfort and safety. If the bed is too high, reduce the height by placing the mattress on a lower, 3-inch (7.5 cm) bed frame instead of the standard 7-inch (18 cm) frame, atop a low-profile box spring, for safer use.

mattresses. They're both hypoallergenic and prevent dust mites.

• **Air.** The unique feature of an air mattress is that it allows you to change the bed's firmness with the push of a button on a hand-held control. The body of the bed is filled with one or two air chambers, depending on whether you sleep solo or not; dual chambers allow you to customize your firmness independently from your partner's. The frame is made with hard foam rails, which give the mattress its shape and stability.

Some people find air mattresses very comfortable, and others complain about "hammock" effects and difficulty finding a comfortable firmness level. A small pump fills the chambers with air; it uses power only when making adjustments, but you'll need an outlet nearby; a surge protector is recommended.

Bed Height

One of the biggest concerns with today's mattresses is the greater height; many new mattresses are 14 inches (35.5 cm) high, an increase of 5 inches (13 cm) from 20 years ago. Some of today's beds are more like thrones, rising as high as 30 inches (76 cm). By contrast, a chair seat is only 18 inches (46 cm) high. A higher bed can be unsafe, especially if you're short. Besides, a luxury bed shouldn't re-

This universal bedroom has vital user-friendly features: abundant lighting, wide doorways with no thresholds, ample space, and a comfortable bed at a safe height.

quire a step stool to use! Stools are not a good option, especially in a dark room.

Whether you're buying a new bed or looking to improve what you have, apply this golden rule: your feet should touch the floor when seated on the bed. If not, you can reduce the bed height either by purchasing a shorter, 3-inch (7.5 cm) metal frame from a bedding company—standard frames are usually 7 inches (18 cm)—and/or by buying a low-profile box spring, typically 5 inches (13 cm) high. The standard height for a box spring is 9 inches (23 cm).

Mattress Overlay Pad

This kind of pad, available in many variations, allows you to change the feel of a bed without the cost of a new mattress. Depending on the condition of the mattress underneath and the thickness of the overlay (thicker is better), the pad may or may not be helpful.

Common overlay pads are made of memory (open-cell) foam, latex foam, or textured foam (like an egg carton). These pads are placed directly on top of the existing mattress, adding 1 to 3 inches (2.5 to 7.5 cm) to the bed height. The higher the pad, the greater the pressure relief.

Mattresses for Couples

My advice is simple: purchase the largest mattress you can afford that your space will accommodate. You'll both sleep more comfortably without the constant threat of flailing elbows and restless legs. Also check out whether the type of mattress you're interested in remains stable when the other person moves—some rock like a ship in a storm and some hardly quiver. Foam mattresses, especially memory foam, transfer less movement than innerspring mattresses, so you're less likely to feel your partner tossing and turning or getting up at night.

Longevity Essentials

Pressure Relief

If you or a loved one has a medical condition that requires a lot of bed rest, a pressure-relieving mattress or overlay surface may help. These can prevent pressure sores, which occur more easily in people who are frail. Many types of materials are available, such as memory foam, gel and foam in combination, and medical grade Australian sheepskin.

But there's no single type that's effective in all situations for all people. For example, some materials (or their plastic covers) make people hot and sweaty. You have to choose especially carefully if you or a family member is at risk for falling. A topper can make the bed higher, which can make transfers more difficult. Plus, some overlays, especially air overlays, have a more unstable transfer surface. That's why it's critical that you talk to your health care professional, especially if the person you care for is frail or has a pressure sore.

If you or a loved one has a medical condition and uses a hospital bed, you already know that standard hospital mattresses are hard. Consider a "pressure relieving" mattress topper to increase comfort and protect the skin.

Streamlined Clothing Storage

You may already have a well-organized closet, with good lighting and clothing neatly tucked away in drawers. But many of us engage in daily battles with crammed, dark closets that require acrobatic stunts to reach anything. Universal design principles can actually rescue you from inconvenient storage and keep you safer. With very little cost and effort, you'll have a place for everything and everything will have its place. You'll also gain the peace of mind that comes with establishing order out of chaos.

Keep in mind that storage needs and organizational systems are very individual, and yours should reflect your personality. You or a family member may never have, nor need to have, all your clothing perfectly lined up, but less clutter and more order will make your bedroom a more spacious and tranquil place to be.

Closet Design Elements

The universal closet has built-in versatility, so you can easily reach your clothing from either a standing or sitting position. If you're renovating your home and adding a walk-in/roll-in closet is an option, be sure it has at least 4 feet (1.2 m) of clear open space and adjustable shelving and poles. If you have a handsome budget and available space, design a "mini-room"

A mix of storage components—drawers, clothing rods at various heights, and pull-out shelving—make this closet a dream come true. Sliding doors free up floor space.

with abundant storage, a comfortable place to sit, and a fold-down ironing board for the occasional touch-up.

Even smaller closets can be transformed from the standard one-size-fits-all design—where the single pole and top shelf reign—to one with double clothes rods and pullout drawers. Then you can easily change the shelving and pole configurations so you can reach your clothes comfortably either standing or sitting.

Whether you use a do-it-yourself shelving and storage system or hire a closet design company to reconfigure the space, these five design principles can help improve the usefulness of any closet, large or small.

1. Simplify & De-Clutter

Put aside a morning and go through your items so you can see what your storage needs really are. Sort the clothes into four piles: clothes worn on a regular basis (bedroom closet); clothes worn infrequently (guest room closet); clothes never worn (charity); and clothes no one should wear (trash bag). Afterward, look at what's left and install more rod space if needed for hanging clothes or more shelf or drawer space for folded clothes.

2. Use Adjustable Rods & Shelves

Serious falls happen unexpectedly when you're standing on a chair or climbing up a ladder, even when you think you're safe. Look into the following, depending on your needs:

• For hanging clothes, use multilevel hanging bars. You can use two rods, one above the other, if the closet is at least 8 feet (2.5 m) high. For high bars, use either a pull-down closet rod or get a long-reach hook to retrieve hangers.

Hang one closet bar about 44 inches (112 cm) from the floor for easy access from a seated position.

• For folded clothes, install pullout shelves, baskets, and drawers. Rearrange your closet so that all shelves are within easy reach (on a level between your shoulder and your waist).

3. Move the Shoes off the Floor

Bending is not only challenging for the less acrobatic, but can cause dizziness in some. Move the shoes off the floor and into a shoe rack or bag. You can buy attractive canvas shoe bags with colorful trim to hang on the inside of the door; or if your closet is large enough, use wire or built-in wooden shelves.

4. Add Lighting

Add or increase closet lighting with either eco-friendly CFL or LED lighting; don't use incandescent bulbs, since they can be a fire hazard in enclosed spaces. Make sure to position the light correctly—between you and the contents of the closet. If it's behind you, you'll cast a shadow on the clothes you're trying to see.

Lighting that turns on when the door opens is a nice convenience feature and especially helpful for people who are memory-impaired. Or you can install a switch on the wall outside the closet.

For a quick fix, add battery-powered LED puck lights that give off bright light; just press the middle of the puck to turn it on and off.

5. Provide Ventilation

Sliding or bifold doors with slats take up less floor space and allow air to pass through, helping to reduce moisture and mildew. Hanging cedar blocks or sachets can protect your clothing from moths and give your closet (or drawers) a fresh scent.

Sliding shelves make it easier to store and reach clothing. The open wire shelving helps to ventilate and keep clothing fresher.

Dressers & Armoires

Since no one design fits all, it's important to customize your clothing storage needs. Choose a taller dresser or armoire if you're tall, especially if bending is a challenge. Or, if you're short or you reach for your clothes while seated, a lower dresser is better. Easily grasped C handles are the most comfortable for everyone, but are especially helpful if you have limited hand agility. Smaller drawers can be easier to open, especially in old dressers that don't have roller glides; if any drawers stick when pulled, rub the slides with a bar of soap or an old candle, which will make opening and closing them much smoother. You may be able to have roller glides installed on heavy or particularly cumbersome drawers, depending on the construction.

This universal bedroom has color-contrasting walls, floors, and fabrics to enhance depth perception. The low-profile bed makes it easier to get in and out of it. The large pulls on the armoire and nightstand allow for easy opening.

Exercising in the Bedroom

If your bedroom is a space you love to be in, why not exercise there? A bedroom is certainly a lot more attractive than the basement or utility room where you may have stashed your seldom-used exercise machine. You don't need a large bedroom or heavy, expensive equipment to reap the benefits of exercise. Even a light workout can increase endurance, balance, and bone density—key ingredients for an active lifestyle. With today's small-sized gear, you can easily store equipment, such as hand weights and resistant bands, in a dresser drawer or on a closet shelf.

If you have a medical condition or you are over age 65 and are not used to regular exercise, consult your physician before beginning a workout.

Design Elements for Your Mini-Gym

It's easy to meet the safety requirements for a gym in your own bedroom. Here are the three key ingredients you need.

1. Exercise mat. A cushioned exercise mat will make the floor (especially if it's wood or tile) more comfortable to lie on. If you're mobile but aren't able to get up from the floor easily, get some individualized tips from a physical therapist on rising with less effort, for example, holding on to a chair for support.

2. Handrail. Install a handrail (well anchored into the wall) if you need a support to hold on to while exercising or stretching.

3. Chair. You can perform many strength-building exercises either sitting in a chair or holding on to the back of one while standing.

Mini-Gym Equipment

The following items are available in a variety of resistances and weights so you can start off easy and progress at your own pace.

• **Stretchable bands.** These easy-to-use rubber or latex strips improve strength and range of motion; the thickness of the band determines the resistance level. Get a set of different bands so you can gradually increase your resistance.

• **Resistant cords.** These rubbery cords, with foam handles for a comfortable grip, give you resistance training to strengthen arms, legs, and torso. Some exercises require you to connect the resistance cords to a doorknob or stand on them; the cord is kept taut when exercising to help strengthen the muscles. The thickness of the tubing determines the resistance level.

• **Vinyl-covered hand weights.** The use of weights improve muscle tone; vinyl is softer to the touch and easier to grip than metal. Plus, they come in fun, bright colors.

• **Cuff weights.** These attach to your wrists or ankles with hook-and-loop tape. When you put them on your ankles, they can increase your leg muscle strength and boost your ability to climb stairs and get up from the floor, which is noticeably more challenging after age 50.

• **Bicycle pedals (without the rest of the bike).** You can ride a "bike" while sitting in a chair to increase leg strength, a key to safe mobility.

It really doesn't take much space or equipment to create a space in the bedroom where you'll look forward to exercising.

A Healing Bedroom

Hospitals today are eager to send patients home as quickly as possible—and with good reason. There is compelling evidence that a comforting and familiar environment promotes wellness. What better environment than your own bedroom? Fortunately, a rapidly growing array of products—including home health technologies that treat and monitor conditions and sensors that send an emergency alert if you haven't left your bed all day—may make it possible for you to live and receive treatments at home, even without a caregiver. Universal design, along with home health equipment, can help with the physical stresses of either receiving or giving medical care at home, making it possible to move about without injury.

To find out more about home care in your community, talk to your doctor, visit AARP's aarp.org/families/caregiving/caring_help/a2003-10-27-caregiving-communityservices.html or contact the National Association for Home Care & Hospice (nahc.org).

Abundant light, greenery, and a warm hearth help create this peaceful bedroom sanctuary. Comfortable furnishings and an uncluttered space add to the room's tranquility.

While most people desire to stay in their homes for the rest of their lives, no one wants a home that looks like a hospital. Beautiful home-care products, like this updated hospital bed designed in warm wood tones and clean lines, are both convenient and pleasing.

Gallery

This bedroom boasts great views and lots of natural light. A remote automatically raises and lowers the shades whenever you desire sun protection, privacy, or bedtime lighting. A deck right off the bedroom is the *pièce de résistance*.

This soothing bedroom has pastel walls to reflect more light and wall-to-wall carpeting for softness underfoot.

Preparing and sharing delicious food with friends and family is one of life's greatest joys. Keeping active, eating well, and connecting with others are also key ingredients for a long, healthy life. Whether you're cooking a simple meal for one or preparing an elaborate holiday dinner for a group, cooking in a universal kitchen helps you (and the other kitchen users) to function at your best.

It's easy to transform a typical kitchen into a flexible and accessible space—without spending a fortune. In this chapter, I'll describe universal design kitchen essentials, such as attractive and safe nonslip flooring. I'll share information about smart and user-friendly cooking appliances, some of which can prevent fires. I'll also discuss energy-efficient lighting that can cheer up any room.

The height of your countertops and the ability to prepare food while sitting down are important topics. We'll look at storage solutions that can make it easier to cook. And if you're ready for your dream makeover, you'll get plenty of inspiration to help you create a gorgeous kitchen—the universal way.

Kitchen Essentials

Kitchens today are more than rooms for cooking. They tend to be the heart of a house and the most appealing living space, where family and visitors gather for conversation and snacking. It's possible that all you need to do to spruce up your kitchen the universal way is make a few simple changes. On the other hand, you might determine that a minor or major remodeling project is in order. For instance, it might be desirable to remove an adjacent room's wall—perhaps the dining room wall—and expand the kitchen or combine the two rooms. This can create a spacious, more user-friendly and inviting eat-in kitchen.

Regardless of the size of the room, the number of people you cook for, or your personal cooking habits, the general workflow is essentially the same in all kitchens. You remove ingredients from the refrigerator, carry them to the sink for washing, move them to a work surface, and then finally place them in a pot on the cooktop or in the oven. Or food is moved from the freezer directly to the microwave or the oven.

Under most circumstances, the ideal design for functionality is either an L-shaped or U-shaped kitchen. The five factors listed here are a good prescription to make the kitchen an easy place to work: consolidated design, easy approach, clear floor space, ease of use, and convenient dining.

This light-filled kitchen has roomy aisle space and a center island for convenient sit-down dining. The microwave built into the island allows for safe handling of hot foods.

Quick Fixes

Two Simple Things

1. Thoreau's advice applies throughout the home, but especially in the kitchen: "Simplify, simplify." Simplify work areas and the entire room as much as possible; organize appliances in one area to reduce unnecessary walking.

2. Sometimes it's not more storage that's needed, but a good cleanout. Hold a tag sale for dishes, cookware, and other kitchen tools that you've accumulated over a lifetime but don't ever use, or give them to an agency that can distribute them to deserving families. You'll be amazed at how much space you gain for everyday items that you really do use.

Sliding wicker baskets set into a base cabinet are an attractive storage option; you can see and get at what you need without having to constantly open and close doors.

Consolidated Design

Design your kitchen around the so-called work triangle, which is formed by the paths connecting the refrigerator, the sink, and the range. Long triangle legs can make meal preparation exhausting, while short ones create a feeling of confinement. A good rule of thumb is that the three legs of the triangle added together shouldn't exceed 22 feet (6.7 m).

Easy Approach

Locate major appliances so they're easy for anyone to get to. For example, place the oven, cooktop, and dishwasher so they all can be approached from right, left, or front, accommodating the cook's natural inclination toward left- or right-handed activity or a person's physically stronger side.

Clear Floor Space

A 30 x 48-inch (76 x 122 cm) area of clear floor space in front of the refrigerator, stove, cooktop, and sink allows a cook who uses a mobility aid much easier access. Similarly, if the kitchen design includes a table or an island in the center, aisles should be 42 to 48 inches wide (107 to 122 cm). This provides room for wheelchairs and walkers, children in strollers, and several cooks. A 5-foot (1.5 m) radius of clear space in the kitchen lets a person using a wheelchair or scooter turn around easily without banging into nearby walls and cabinets or having to back his or her way out of the room.

This streamlined kitchen has a spacious floor area for easy movement, under-cabinet lighting for safer food preparation, a smooth cooktop for simplified cleanup, and upper cabinets installed lower than usual for a more comfortable reach.

This kitchen offers open floor space for mobility aids and generous space for two cooks. The eco-friendly linoleum flooring and bright countertop colors are easily distinguished, helping those with visual impairments.

Ease of Use

Universal design makes cooking tasks easier, not harder. For example, the longer the unbroken work surfaces and the closer the sink is to the cooktop and oven, the more flexibility you'll have in preparing food. This also means less moving of ingredients or lifting of heavy pots or food since you can easily slide them along the counter. Your back will be happier, too.

Convenient Dining

Plan your kitchen so it's easy to serve and eat meals. For instance, a dining table or an eat-in counter on a kitchen island is a real plus for casual, relaxed meals. And it also saves having to walk with hands laden with plates, cups, and serving dishes. An easy option is to install a pullout tray under the countertop to serve as a table for dining solo, or add a hinged extension leaf on your island. Another low-cost solution is to purchase a small wheeled cart. It makes transporting food from the kitchen to the table much easier.

A pass-through window between the kitchen and dining area is a great convenience feature. Add folding wooden shutters and you have a camouflaged pass-through when it's not in use.

A kitchen pass-through window can be elegant as well as practical, allowing food and dinnerware to be passed either way. The kitchen countertop extending into the adjacent room makes a great spot for a buffet or an open bar.

This dining table with a view offers a convenient (and luxurious) sit-down spot for meal preparation. Family and friends can also enjoy a meal here.

Lighting & Electrical

Good lighting can do wonders for any kitchen. It makes all the kitchen surfaces more visible, which is important because you'll feel more secure and safe as you prepare and cook food. Good lighting can also make small spaces seem larger. Plus, adequate light can create a sense of well being.

Light It Up!

A well-illuminated kitchen has two types of lighting: general lighting, the overall illumination that comes from daylight or from overhead fixtures, and task-specific lighting. Both are important in the kitchen.

When it comes to general lighting, a large ceiling fixture with long-lasting eco-friendly fluorescent bulbs will give off plenty of light and mean fewer trips up and down a ladder.

Lighter colors for the walls and cabinetry reflect more light. A good mix of indoor lighting, such as recessed downlights and under-cabinet lights, helps you see and function better.

Abundant lighting throughout this kitchen—including recessed ceiling lights and under-cabinet and range-hood lighting—makes meal preparation and cooking safer.

You can improve task lighting by installing fluorescent fixtures under the cabinets or by adding lighting over the range, sink, and other areas where much of your work takes place.

Electrical Plan

It's essential to install an electrical system that is safe and easy to use. The number and placement of outlets is especially important in a kitchen—for ease of use and to satisfy current building codes. A good, inexpensive strategy is to install a surface-mounted cable raceway at the back of the counter or under the cabinets to make more outlets available for small appliances. All outlets, especially those near water, must be changed to ground-fault-interrupter outlets, known as GFI outlets, to avoid the possibility of shock. And remember to install your light switches and electrical outlets no higher than 48 inches (122 cm) from the floor for easy reach.

This pop-up counter near a convenient outlet keeps the countertop uncluttered and gives you an additional work surface when using small appliances.

Watch the Cords!

If you must use extension cords, select only those with built-in circuit breakers. The thickness, or gauge, of the wire is what determines extension cord ratings. Many cords are intended for use only with table lamps, and present a fire hazard when used for kitchen appliances with a heavy electrical draw. Read the gauge of the wire on the extension cord tab to see if it's adequate for the appliance you have in mind.

Keep It Current

Relocate your fuse box or service panel from a hard-to-access location (like the basement) to a place you can reach easily in your kitchen or a nearby hallway. And update your service panel. Most older homes have a 60-amp service panel, although the minimum used today is 100 amps. Current safety codes require separate circuits for appliances such as microwaves and refrigerators. If you're renovating your kitchen, ask your electrician about the need to upgrade the electrical power and whether worn-out insulation around the wiring should be replaced at the same time.

Quick Fixes

Under-Cabinet Lighting

One of the easiest and least expensive ways to boost the appeal of any kitchen is to install under-cabinet lighting. You can purchase energy-efficient fluorescent fixtures that flood the countertop with warm, even lighting; consider plug-in models that don't require wiring—just attach the unit to the bottom of the cabinet and plug in the cord. These fixtures put light right where you need it, are reasonably priced, and are readily available at local home stores. Other types of lighting, including LED strip lighting or puck lights, have narrow, spotty beams of light rather than the wide, even illumination you get from fluorescents.

Here are three tips for getting the most out of fluorescent lighting:

1. To obtain good, even lighting on the countertops, choose the largest fluorescent fixture that will fit under the upper cabinet.

2. Install the fixture in the recessed space under the upper cabinet, close to the front of the cabinet.

3. If your cabinets don't have a valance and/or the fixture hangs down too far, so that the light shines into the eyes of someone seated, add a trim to the bottom of the cabinets.

This under-cabinet lighting throws even lighting on the countertop, making kitchen chores safer and easier.

Kitchen Appliances

There was a time when the choice in kitchen appliances was limited to color and size. Today, there are so many products available that deciding which to install can be more confusing than liberating! From drawer refrigerators to fancy countertop cooktops with woks, griddles, and other gizmos, the array of appliances can be overwhelming. It can also make it hard to separate fact from marketing fiction.

The good news is that many of the latest appliances, especially cooktops and ovens, combine style with enhanced safety features—demonstrating the universal design concept that improved function can be beautiful.

I've done quite a bit of homework in this area so that I can put you in a better position to decide what appliances and gadgets make sense for you and your kitchen. Read on to learn about the latest cooking technologies and design features that can help conserve energy and increase safety and efficiency.

Here are three general pieces of advice:

1. Regardless of the appliance, brand, or model you're interested in, look for large-sized buttons and controls in bright, contrasting colors. They minimize mistakes with the controls.

2. When buying new appliances, select "quiet" models that are well insulated. For example, choose your refrigerator, range hood, dishwasher, and even your blender with care, as noisy models can sound like jet engines, even to those with hearing loss.

3. Available in electric, induction, or gas, ceramic glass cooktops are attractive and easy to clean. But note that these surfaces can scratch or mark (for example, when sliding rough pan bottoms). Also, they can be damaged if you forcefully set down a pot or drop an item like a knife, spice bottle, or soup can onto the cooktop. (So don't store anything above the cooktop.)

When planning your new kitchen, design for a lifetime of changing needs. Build in as much flexibility as possible and put everything within easy reach.

easy to go green
Energy-Efficient Appliances

By choosing energy-efficient appliances, you're helping to prevent global warming and promote cleaner air. And you get to save on utility bills. Since green isn't associated with any style or model, you don't have to sacrifice aesthetics, quality, or performance. Good for you, good for the environment.

LEARN MORE AT energystar.gov

Appliances labeled "Energy Star" are certified energy-efficient by the U.S. government. Unfortunately, *Consumer Reports* discovered that some refrigerators used almost twice the amount of energy reported. The Energy Star program has lapsed, with out-of-date tests, old technology, and a policy of letting manufacturers do their own testing. Until this program is revamped, consumers should look for supplemental sources of information.

Refrigerators & Freezers

The refrigerator is the biggest energy-consuming appliance in the kitchen. If you have an older model, it's using up to twice as much electricity as an energy-efficient one. The U.S. Department of Energy reports that replacing a refrigerator bought in 1990 with an energy-efficient model saves enough power to light the average household for nearly four months! New features, like high-efficiency compressors and improved insulation, will not only lower your utility bills but will also reduce your carbon footprint.

If you're in the market for a new refrigerator, consider a side-by-side model if it fits your kitchen. It makes it easy to grab both fresh and frozen goods without excessive bending or reaching. And the smaller size doors don't swing out as far as larger single doors do—a real plus in a busy kitchen. Most refrigerators come with pullout shelves, but in the more upscale models you'll find additional features, such as an express thaw that allows you to thaw a frozen meal for dinner in a couple of hours; special cooling zones that keep foods

The lower work surface, with plenty of comfortable legroom, allows you to prepare meals or have a snack while seated. The side-by-side refrigerator offers convenient access to both fresh and frozen food.

fresher and crisper for longer; and bright LED lighting that makes food easier to see. And yes, there are even refrigerators installed in pullout drawers, usually under the countertop, for convenience and extra storage space during holiday parties. Such a unit is pricey, but if you host large get-togethers, it just may be worth splurging on.

What features can you expect to see in the near future? New refrigerators will use Internet capability and barcode-scanning technology to keep track of your food items and send an e-mail reorder to your local store. When you arrive home from work at 6:00 P.M., your groceries will arrive shortly after you do (like magic).

This consolidated kitchen has an eat-in counter and cork flooring with a matte finish. In a small room, a refrigerator with a top or bottom freezer can be a good choice.

easy to go green
Refrigerators

If you follow these simple steps, your refrigerator will operate more efficiently:

• Don't place the refrigerator next to the oven, the dishwasher, or in sunlight—these locations overwork the unit.

• Keep the back or bottom coils clean.

• Leave a space between the wall and the condenser coils to allow air to circulate.

• Make sure the door seals are airtight. You may need to replace them on older refrigerators.

• Buy a thermometer and check the temperature. The U.S. Department of Agriculture recommends a setting of 35° to 40°F (2° to 4°C) for the refrigerator and 0°F (-18°C) for the freezer.

• Don't hold the refrigerator door open for too long. Good storage organization will decrease the time it takes to search for items.

• Recycle your old refrigerator if you're buying a new one. Go to earth911.com to find the nearest refrigerator recycling location.

An eco–friendly water and ice dispenser on the door reduces the number of times you have to open the refrigerator.

Longevity Essentials

Healthy Eating

Eating the right kinds of food can not only make you feel and function better, but it can actually prevent disease. Healthy eating may reduce the risk of heart disease, stroke, type 2 diabetes, bone loss, some kinds of cancer, and anemia. And if you already have one or more of these conditions, healthy eating, along with physical activity, may help you better manage them.

A healthy diet can also be a delicious one, rich in vegetables and fruits, whole grains, high-fiber foods, lean meats and poultry, Omega-3 fish, and low-fat dairy products. Whatever your age, eating well can help you stay healthier and more independent—and look and feel good—in the years to come.

For more information, check out aarp.org/health/healthyliving and from the National Institutes of Health nihseniorhealth.gov/eatingwellasyougetolder/toc.html.

Whipping up healthy, delicious meals is more enjoyable when there is generous space to move about, comfortable flooring, and good meal prep tools.

Cooking Appliances

Until a decade ago, the "all-in-one range," with burners on top and the oven underneath, was the only game in town. Today, the many advantages of separate cooktops and wall ovens have made them popular.

First, your back will thank you. Instead of reaching and groping into a hot oven, a wall-mounted oven can be installed at a height that allows safe, easy, and direct access. Second, with separate units, you can install the cooktop near the food prep area—in the countertop or the island—at a convenient height. And third, if there's more than one cook at a time in your household, one person can use the cooktop free and clear without having to dodge oven doors and large hot pans coming and going. Be sure that both appliances have generous countertop space on both sides for setting down hot dishes and the like.

Most standard wall ovens are electric and self-cleaning. Select a side-opening door so you can get at the interior of the oven easily, and install a heat-resistant pullout shelf under the oven where you can set down hot pans. Install the oven, depending on your needs, so its base is 29 to 34 inches (73.5 to 86 cm) above the floor.

If you don't have the room for a separate cooktop and wall oven, however, the freestanding all-in-one range is a good choice. Today's options include gas and electric, or even a combination of these; in addition, you can get an induction cooktop (see pages 135 to 137). When choosing a range, you'll want to look for controls located on the top front surface, and a lockout safety feature that allows you to disable the oven and burner controls (good for young children or adults with memory loss).

Using an energy-efficient induction cooktop is one of the safest ways to cook. There is no hot coil, open flame, or even a heated surface—only the pan is heated.

Select a model with a large, clear glass window and good interior lighting; this helps you see the food cooking without having to open the oven, an eco-friendly feature.

Rating the Safety of Cooking Technology

The main types of cooking technologies are electric, induction, and gas, and each has its pros and cons. Now they can be combined. Safety, energy efficiency, and, of course, easy cleanup are important features, but for everyone—young, old, and in-between—safety is the biggest concern. More household fires start in the kitchen than in any other place in the home—and *unattended* cooking is the leading cause of home fires. Two new products on the market—low-temperature electric burners and induction cooktops—perform quite well without an open flame or red-hot cooking elements. These new technologies can help you or an older parent stay safe in the kitchen.

This listing of cooking technologies is presented in order of safety, from low-temperature electric burners and induction through electric and gas. Note that though the first two are about equal in safety, low-temperature electric is substantially less expensive than induction.

Electric: Low-Temperature Burners

Low-temperature electric burners are cast-iron plates that are one-third to one-half as hot as regular electric burners; the maximum temperature on these plates is 662°F (350°C) compared to a whopping 1400°F (760°C) on a standard electric burner. They're hot enough to boil water and cook delicious meals but not hot enough for oil, food, and most household materials (like pot holders, clothing, and paper) to ignite. You can purchase

A rail firmly anchored into the countertop edge functions as a support for anyone with balance problems.

a new cooktop or a range with these low-temperature burners already installed, or you can hire a technician to install them over your existing coiled burners. An added bonus: these burners are eco-friendly because they use less energy.

Because the burner plates do remain hot to the touch longer than standard elements after the power is off, consider buying a cooktop that has indicator lights to remind you that the elements may still be hot. This low-temperature technology scores high for healthy longevity: it can save lives. The burner plates are relatively affordable—purchasing a cooktop or stove with the burners already installed does not add substantially to the price.

Induction

Although this radically different cooking technology was launched in 1933 at the World's Fair in Chicago, it has become popular only in the last decade—primarily in Europe and Asia. Induction is now making inroads into the U.S. market because its benefits are safety and energy efficiency.

Induction differs from other cooking processes in that there is no hot coil, open flame, or heated surface. Instead, it uses a coil of copper wire just below the cooktop's glass ceramic surface; when an electric current is passed through this wire, it heats the *cookware* directly through the magnetic field it creates, making it the most efficient and greenest cooktop available. Only the area under the cookware gets hot; the copper coil itself doesn't get hot and the unused portion of the cooktop remains relatively cool. It's this absence of a hot heating element or flame that gives induction its extra margin of safety. But the surface *under* the pan does get hot (from contact with the pan)—hot enough to cause a burn.

If you're concerned about the electromagnetic energy that creates the heat in the cookware, you can relax; it's what we're surrounded by all day in the form of radio and television waves, Wi-Fi hot spots, and microwave ovens. Speaking of safety, if you have a pacemaker, check with your doctor before using induction—the same precaution you should take with microwave ovens.

IT'S WISE TO BE SAFE

Induction Safety Features

1. Two types of automatic turn off:

– An integrated timer that can set a cooking time for each burner; when the timer goes off, the burner automatically powers off.

– A maximum cooking time; some models automatically shut off after two hours.

2. A residual-heat indicator light to alert you if the cooktop is still hot to the touch after being turned off.

3. Turn-off feature/pan detector that powers off the cooktop if a burner is turned on without placing a pan on it or if the pan is empty.

Low-temperature burners provide ample heat to cook a meal, but not at the high temperatures of regular burners that are more likely to cause a fire.

Induction has a response time similar to that of a gas stove and is much faster than any other type of electric cooking. Induction cooking is approximately 83 percent energy efficient, compared to gas and electric at 50 to 60 percent. And induction doesn't throw off a lot of heat into the kitchen, a real bonus when the weather is warm. It's also an easy cleanup since the cooktop doesn't get hot enough to burn any spills or drips.

But cooking with induction may take some getting used to, especially if you've been depending on flame size to judge the level of heat. With induction, just as with electric cooktops, you have only a marked knob with LED numbers and an indicator light. Also, induction cooktops are expensive: they cost at least twice as much as gas or electric models. But keep in mind you'll reduce your electricity bill.

In addition to the higher initial cost, there is another potentially daunting trade-off. You can use only flat-bottomed cookware made of magnetic materials, such as cast-iron and most stainless steel. If a refrigerator magnet sticks firmly to the bottom of the pan, you're OK. If not, you'll need to buy new cookware. Look for cookware (thicker bottoms will heat more evenly) that is specifically made for induction cooking. The increased safety may be well worth the additional investment in cookware, depending on your situation.

A retractable vent hood removes odors and cooking pollutants from an island cooktop. When not in use, the vent slides back into the cabinet.

If you're curious about induction and wonder if it's the right cooking technology for your household, you can purchase a relatively inexpensive one-burner hot plate and test it. It can always be put to good use as an extra cooktop in the kitchen (or even in the dining or family room) to warm up food during family gatherings and holiday parties.

Standard Electric

Available with either coiled burners or a glass ceramic surface, electric cooktops and ovens have heating elements under the surface. The heating elements turn red, a visual aid for safety and useful if you have low vision or like strong visual reminders. However, unlike their low-temperature counterparts, standard electric burners can reach very high temperatures, and, as with gas burners, you need to be extremely careful not to let loose-fitting or hanging garments, newspapers, pot holders, and other fire hazards come into contact with the burner.

Gas

If you're used to cooking on a gas stove, you appreciate the fast heat, precise temperature control (simmer, low, high, and everything in between), and the ability to judge the cooking temperature by the size of the flame.

But there are some major safety issues, especially for young children and older adults. The open flame presents serious burn and fire risks, especially if you're wearing long sleeves while cooking. Leaving a gas burner on or having a flame extinguished accidentally by a strong gust of wind can cause problems, a concern for older adults who have a decreased sense of smell. These hazards can make converting from gas to induction or electric technology well worth it, even if it requires you to upgrade your electrical system.

Gas cooktops are good for fast cooking, but the open flame can increase fire risk. Explore safer options, such as induction stoves and low-temperature electric burners.

IT'S WISE TO BE SAFE

Electric Cooktop Safety Features

• An automatic turn-off feature that shuts down the cooktop if an object, such as an oven mitt, covers the touch controls or a burner is left on and there's no pot or pan.

• A combination timer and turn-off feature that allows you to set a cooking time for each burner; when the timer goes off, the burner automatically powers off.

• A residual-heat indicator light that alerts you if the cooktop is still hot to the touch.

IT'S WISE TO BE SAFE

Gas Cooktop Safety Features

If you're determined to cook with gas, make it as safe as possible. Insist on these safety features:

• Continuous (not individual) grates that allow smooth movement of cookware to reduce lifting and spilling.

• Lock-out features that make turning on the cooktop impossible for young children and adults with memory loss.

• Reigniting burners that automatically relight if the flame goes out accidentally.

Wall Ovens

Most standard wall ovens are electric and self-cleaning. The more expensive models offer convection cooking, which speeds up cooking time. This is a feature you may or may not require, depending on your cooking habits. Ovens do not receive an Energy Star rating; choose a model with a large clear glass window and good interior lighting. This allows you to see the food cooking without having to open the oven—you'll save energy and help the environment.

To upgrade to a truly universal design wall oven, select one with a side-opening door, so you can get at the inside easily. You can install a heat-resistant pullout shelf under the oven on which to set down hot pans. When you install the oven, raise the base so it's 29 to 34 inches (73.5 to 86 cm) above the floor, depending on your needs.

The latest trend for wall ovens is an "oven in a drawer." If you have a hefty budget and often host large get-togethers, you can install convenient warming drawers in any room of your house to keep food appetizingly warm.

Wall-mounted ovens let more than one person cook because the cooktop is in a separate part of the kitchen. A side-opening door allows you to get closer to the oven without reaching. A pull-out shelf below is a handy surface for hot dishes.

This cooktop has legroom for a seated user, but note that cooking while sitting requires special safety precautions. Microwave ovens installed on or under the countertop are safer and more convenient.

Microwave Ovens

New microwave ovens are easier to use than ever, with shortcut keys and sensors that cook a variety of dishes, from pasta to steamed veggies. When buying a new microwave, the biggest decisions you'll need to make are the size and the type of unit you need, which have everything to do with your kitchen size and the kind of meals you prepare. You may not need all the bells and whistles if you use the microwave only for reheating leftovers and making popcorn. A compact microwave may be your best bet, especially if you have a small kitchen. These ovens use around 800 watts and take a little longer to cook than a larger model. Keep in mind that some compact models have such small interiors that you can't even cook two small potpies at the same time.

If you cook for two or more people, or use the microwave to whip up entire meals, then you'll want at least a mid-size oven with 1200 to 1500 watts and the latest innovations, like a convection feature (a fan and a bulb), which not only speeds up the cooking but also provides browning and crisping—important if you're fond of crispy pizza or roasted chicken. Large-size models are designed for large dishes like casseroles or turkey breast—and for large kitchens. These powerful ovens use more than 2000 watts; they are over 20 inches (51 cm) wide, 20 inches (51 cm) deep, and 12 inches (30.5 cm) high, and they are often built into the cabinetry like traditional ovens.

Regardless of size, for fast, easy cooking, choose a microwave with sensors that automatically set the temperature and cooking time and then turn off the microwave when the food is cooked. Before too long, microwaves will be able to read the bar code on frozen or packaged items and automatically set the cooking time.

IT'S WISE TO BE SAFE

Safe Microwave Use

Hot drinks and dishes can easily spill and scald when removed from a microwave, especially if it's installed under an upper cabinet. A rule of thumb is that you shouldn't remove hot items at face level or above. For the best handling of hot food, install the microwave on a countertop with adjacent counter space where you can set down hot dishes quickly and comfortably. But if you have little counter space or are using a microwave while sitting, purchase a built-in microwave and mount it on a wall or under the countertop.

Choose a microwave oven with built-in sensors to take the guesswork out of cooking. By pushing a button or two, you can automatically set the temperature and cooking time.

Range hoods pull out cooking odors and steam and let fresh air come in. Choose a hood that's at least as wide as the cooking surface, with built-in downlights, and as quiet a fan as you can afford.

IT'S WISE TO BE SAFE

Gas & Carbon Monoxide Detectors

Gas leaks. If you're using propane or natural gas, be sure to use a gas detector to alert you to a leak. This will prevent dangerous levels of gas from building up—and possibly causing an explosion. Even though a "rotten egg" chemical is added to gas to help with detection, our sense of smell gradually declines with age, so many of us won't notice a gas leak without a detector.

Carbon monoxide. Carbon monoxide (CO) poisoning is the leading cause of accidental poisoning deaths in the United States. Because it's odorless and invisible, the only sure way to know if carbon monoxide is present is to install a CO detector.

Hint: You can get a three-in-one detector that covers propane, natural gas, and carbon monoxide.

Stove Range Hoods

The range hood is an important part of your kitchen design. It helps maintain good indoor air quality by sucking out contaminants, heat, and odors. Like stovetops and ovens, hoods come in a wide "range" of styles and have different features. To ensure your choice is safe and user-friendly, select a model with radius, or rounded corners. Hang it no lower than 56 inches (142 cm) from the floor. Downdraft models are good for grilling and frying; updraft models, for the evacuation of steam. The size and type of fan used in the hood determines the noise level (and the differences are large), so be sure to listen to the unit you're considering before leaving the showroom. For added safety, an automatic fire-suppressant system can be purchased separately and installed in most hoods at little additional cost.

Dishwashers

As with any appliance, when it comes to dishwashers you want performance, energy efficiency, and convenience. Dishwasher efficiency has improved dramatically in the past decade as new soil sensors determine both the wash cycle time and the water temperature needed to clean the dishes. And that's not all. Better pumps, filtration systems, rotating jets, and pressurized spray nozzles get dishes cleaner, with less water, and—you'll really appreciate this—with no prescrubbing. Some models even allow you to run a half load with less water, a real plus for someone living alone. Choose a dishwasher with a quiet motor that makes it possible for everyone to hold a conversation while the dishes are being washed. Now if only it came with robots to load the dishwasher!

The universal design approach is to install the dishwasher on a plat-

A raised dishwasher requires less bending and straining.

form at a back-friendly height, about 9 inches (23 cm) from the floor. For increased storage space, you can install a drawer in the platform for seldom-used items. There is a trade-off, though: because the counter on top of the dishwasher will be higher than the adjacent one, you won't be able to slide pots and pans across the countertop easily, an inconvenience when moving heavy pots. As always, choose what's best for your situation.

Sinks

From meal prep to cleanup, the sink is an essential element in any kitchen. You can choose one that has ergonomic features, such as adjustable height and easy-to-operate faucets. Where you place the sink—remember, it's one of the key components in the "work triangle"—largely determines how efficiently and easily the cook (or cooks) can move around the kitchen.

easy to go green
Dishwashers

Most of the energy used by a dishwasher goes to heating the water. So if you're using an older dishwasher, run it only with a full load. Newer, eco-friendly models let you reduce the amount of water used for smaller loads. Another energy-saving measure: skip the dry cycle and let dishes air-dry.

This spacious kitchen has two sinks. The main sink, installed under a beautiful picture window next to the dishwasher, and the island sink are far enough apart that several cooks can easily work together.

So where should you place the sink? A pleasant spot is under a window that lets daylight in. Hang a bird feeder right outside, and you won't mind meal prep or cleanup as much. Just make sure you have adequate counter space on both sides and that you can easily open the dishwasher door when you're at the sink, a good reason why you *shouldn't* install a sink in a corner location. You'll also find that if you frequently have multiple cooks, two sinks in a kitchen is very handy, if you have the room. But place them far enough apart to prevent traffic congestion.

Sink Height

Both meal prep and wash up will be more enjoyable if your body is in a relaxed, nonstrained position. Depending on your situation, there are several ways to install the sink so it's at a back-friendly height.

One option is a push-button, adjustable-height sink that gives each user a custom fit. The good news is that any sink or countertop you select can be raised and lowered from 28 to 40 inches (71 to 101.5 cm) with the simple push of a button; the motor is installed under the sink. This is ideal if you have a partner who is much taller or shorter than you or for anyone who prefers to sit when at the sink. (Your partner will have no more *legitimate* excuses for not doing the dishes!)

An alternative is to install the sink in a countertop at a fixed height that's comfortable for you now but allows for adjustments later on. For maximum flexibility, select a shallow sink, approximately 5 to 6½ inches (12.5 to 16.5 cm) deep, with a drain in the rear. If this brings up images of an unattractive, institutional-like kitchen, think again! You'll be delighted to know you can have flexibility with beauty.

It's a good idea to use flexible, plastic plumbing lines rather than rigid PVC pipes; they'll give you the option of raising or lowering the sink with less effort later on. If you want to design the sink so that you can sit rather than stand, remember that the pipes must be insulated, along with the bottom of the sink. You can hide unsightly plumbing behind a panel—but attach the panel so it can be easily removed.

An adjustable-height sink gives you instant flexibility to meet the needs of different users. Just push a button to lower or raise the sink. This design has cabinet doors that slide out of the way, a shallow sink, flexible tubing, and a finished floor under the cabinet.

Faucets & Handles

A single-lever handle (as opposed to knobs) is the best universal design choice, because most people can use it easily—even those with arthritis. But if you prefer individual handles, choose a model with two levers (one for hot water, the other for cold). If you don't want to actually replace the existing faucets, look for a lever faucet adapter.

Electronic faucets free up your hands—and they're safer too, reducing contamination if you have, say, raw chicken on your hands. But there are trade-offs. Some models turn on when you walk by—not so good for the environment. And the water temperature is usually set for an average temperature, so you don't get very cold or very hot water unless you make special adjustments, which isn't always easy to do.

Another universal design idea is to install a faucet with a long hose that lets you fill a pot on a nearby cooktop without having to lift it. Be sure to measure how far away the cooktop is from the faucet, as hose lengths range from 22 to 60 inches (56 to 152.5 cm). Some cooks install a pot-filler faucet right by the cooktop—you'll always have cooking water right where it's needed.

You can also install a hot water dispenser, which is a great convenience for anyone living alone who frequently makes soup or tea. The standard temperature setting is 190°F (88°C), but it can be adjusted. A word of caution: hot water dispensers can be dangerous for anyone with memory impairment. (Hot water, of course, is a safety issue in the kitchen and the bathroom. See Prevent Scalding in chapter 8, page 171.)

easy to go green
Saving Water

Install automatically timed faucets that turn off the water within 10 to 20 seconds if it's left running. This type of faucet is recommended for a person with dementia who may forget to turn off the faucets.

Here's another example of how universal design helps everyone. A pot filler at the stove or cooktop allows you to fill a pot right where you need it, reducing the need to carry heavy pots to the stove.

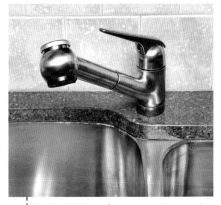

A single-lever faucet requires only one hand to mix the water temperature and control the volume.

Countertops

Whether you've had a long day at the office or are recovering from foot surgery, most of us have wished, at one time or another, that we could chop vegetables while sitting down. With universal design's built-in flexibility, you can devise a countertop that will work whether you sit or stand.

Counter Height

The height of any work surface is one of the most important factors in creating a comfortable space. It's a great idea to have at least two different countertop heights—the standard 36 inches (91.5 cm), if this height works for you, and a lower height of 30 inches (76 cm)—so you, a friend, or a grand-child can work while seated. Standard base cabinets are 34½ inches (87.5 cm) tall, which includes a 4-inch (10 cm) toe kick space. Countertop material adds another 1½ inches (4 cm), bringing the standard kitchen work surface to 36 inches (91.5 cm). The ideal countertop height is typically 6 inches (15 cm) below your elbow, as measured

This kitchen was featured in the first designer showhouse for universal design in Atlanta, Georgia (2006). Highlights include countertops and surfaces at different heights, such as the extended table for sit-down dining or meal preparation.

The universal kitchen has multiple countertop heights to suit a variety of needs for grandchildren, grandparents, and everyone in between. The lower countertop is at an ideal height for baking prep, like kneading bread or pizza dough.

Quick Fixes

Ergonomic Shortcuts

If kitchen renovation is not a viable option, you can create a lower work surface by installing a hinged extension leaf on a kitchen island or on a wall at an ergonomic work height of 30 to 32 inches (76 to 81 cm)—whatever suits you best. An even easier solution is to place a cutting board on top of an open kitchen drawer (as long as the drawer is stable!).

while you're standing, so adjust accordingly. The most ergonomic countertop height for those cooking while seated is 30 to 32 inches (76 to 81 cm). This is also a great surface height for kneading dough while standing, baking cookies with grandchildren, or using your laptop to find a favorite recipe.

To take advantage of sitting while working in the kitchen, keep a section of your countertop—a 3-foot (91.5 cm) wide space is nice—with room for your knees underneath. If you're reluctant to give up the storage space, designate one base cabinet for possible removal later; the floor surface under this cabinet should be finished, as should be the sides of the adjacent cabinets. Screw the countertop of this section of cabinetry into the wall (not into the base cabinets If the need arises, all you have to do is remove the cabinet (no tearing up the kitchen), for a customized, comfortable, and functional workspace.

A perfect chair for meal prep at the sink or countertop is a perching stool. Look for one with side arms, a comfy padded backrest, and an adjustable-height, slightly slanted seat that makes getting on and off easier and safer. If the best place to sit doesn't allow you to tuck in your legs, see if you can remove an under-the-counter cupboard door.

Materials

You can make all kitchen countertops function better by selecting the proper surface material. Fortunately, with today's choices, you don't have to sacrifice aesthetics for practicality.

When shopping for countertops, look for durable, even surface materials. Avoid options, such as tile, that may be pleasing to the eye but aren't completely level. And keep in mind that, with the exception of stainless steel or stone, most surfaces can't withstand the heat of pots taken directly from the oven or the burner. But don't worry. You can avoid damaging your countertop by using an array of trivets or metal grills. If you choose a laminate countertop, specify a "no-drip" edge. This ⅛-inch (3 mm) lip around all or part of the countertop will reduce spills and floor clean-up jobs.

A clever universal design idea is to choose a countertop that's a different color from the cabinets, and use a colorful border on the edges. This arrangement makes the countertop pop visually, which is especially important for those with visual impairments. Choosing a relatively light shade for your countertop means it'll be easier to see food and utensils.

Granite countertops offer an attractive, durable, and heat-resistant surface. Specify rounded edges for safety's sake.

Cabinets

Most people never complain that their kitchen has *too* much storage space. It seems that no matter how much cabinet space you have, you'll eventually find a sufficient quantity of pots and cooking gadgets to fill it. It's also true that sometimes this storage space is useless because it's so difficult to reach. Here's a storage tip: place frequently used tableware, cookware, and food within easy reach and store everything else on higher shelves.

Cabinet Height

In a universal kitchen, upper cabinets are hung on commercial brackets so that height adjustments can be made at a later date. Isn't that smart? The standard cabinet height is 18 to 24 inches (46 to 61 cm) from the countertop, but a 15-inch (38 cm) height makes the second shelf easier to reach for a person of average height while still allowing ample room for countertop appliances, such as microwaves, toasters, and most blenders.

Cabinet Design

If you're replacing your cabinets as part of your universal design update, keep accessibility as your main criterion, both in terms of the cabinets' design and the way they're mounted on the wall. There are many cabinet designs and arrangements that can fulfill this goal with style. In general, however, frameless cabinets provide more storage space for small kitchens.

Cabinet doors can be a mixture of wood and glass (making it easy

For easier access, these sleek kitchen cabinets are hung lower than usual. The base cabinets feature a mix of sliding drawers and interior shelves for various storage needs. The partial wall supports an eat-in countertop and opens up views into the kitchen; it also creates additional storage space.

to see what's on the shelves), or in some cases the doors are removed altogether, making it much easier to reach into the cabinets. This can also be aesthetically pleasing—but only if the cabinets showcase well-organized tableware. (If you choose the open option, you'll need an adequate range-hood fan to make sure grease from the kitchen air is removed and doesn't collect on the dishes.) Another nice feature is touch magnetic latches that allow you to open cabinet doors using minimal strength. If you're using nonmagnetic latches, colorful C handles are the best choice because they are easy to grasp. Another practi-

These bamboo cabinets have plenty of storage room, including the extra space in the island, and an appliance garage keeps the countertop uncluttered.

easy to go green
Countertops & Cabinets

Here are some eco-friendly materials that make great cabinets and countertops. Because products can look very different in a showroom or in a magazine, it's always a good idea to request samples to see how well they work with your other finishes—under your actual kitchen lighting.

Cabinets

• Choose formaldehyde-free particleboard or fiberboard, such as wheat-board panels, which is made from the remnants of the straw waste left over from farmers' wheat crops, milled and bound together with formaldehyde-free binders. It's very strong, exceeding the set standards for particleboard in North America.

• Use water-based paints, primers, adhesives, and finishes with either no- or low-volatile organic compounds (VOCs).

• Choose woods from renewable sources, such as bamboo, or from recycled materials.

• Look for the seal from the Forest Stewardship Council (FSC), an active voice in green cabinetry.

Countertops

• Use terrazzo-like recycled glass and concrete. They're durable, heat-resistant, and available in a wide array of colors. Currently, you can get terrazzo only in a high-gloss surface, but you can hire an outside workshop to refinish it to a matte, non-shiny surface to reduce glare.

• Choose a local stone—for example, quartz, slate, or granite.

• Select a laminate made from recycled, formaldehyde-free products with low-emitting substrates, low-VOC glues, or mechanical fasteners.

This beautiful and eco-friendly kitchen features rich honey-toned bamboo cabinets and concrete countertops.

cal option is a knife hinge; this allows cabinet doors to be folded back flush (at 180°), eliminating the need to duck when the doors are open.

Mobile shelving is a good choice, too: it's adaptable and brings hard-to-reach items to your fingertips. You can purchase pull-down shelving, avail-able in 24- and 36-inch (61 and 91.5 cm) widths, for your upper cabinets. In your lower cabinets, pullout shelves and drawers on full extension glides, lazy Susans, and pop-up shelves for appliances can expand usable storage space and reduce bending and reach-ing toward the back of the shelf.

The beauty of universal design is its built-in flex-ibility to adapt to chang-ing needs. Even if you don't need a sit-down workspace now, you can remove this cabinet later. Because the floor-ing and sidewalls are already finished, no additional remodeling is necessary.

This pull-down shelf mechanism brings items stored in the upper cabinets within easy reach.

A sliding panty installed under the cabinet organizes items and brings them into easy reach.

IT'S WISE TO BE SAFE

Kitchen Fires

Did you know that most home fires start in the kitchen due to unattended cooking? Because this room presents more hazards, you need safety products that can help prevent a fire from ever starting, warn you of one in pro-cess, and extinguish the flames safely and efficiently. Here are some ways you can make sure your kitchen is a safe place to be.

Preventing a Fire

• Use a portable timer with a long, loud ring that can be taken with you to different rooms or that you can hear from another room. Most kitchen fires start because cooking food is left forgotten on the stove when the phone rings in another room, or when the cook begins a different activity somewhere else in the house. Some people like to wear a timer around their neck.

• Use an electric teakettle that shuts off automatically when the water boils.

• Install an automatic shut-off timer on electric stoves to reduce the possibility that unattended or forgotten pots might start a fire.

• Use low-temperature electric burners or an induction cooktop.

• Use only those appliances that have timers and auto turn-off features.

Smoke & Fire Warning

• Smoke alarms are a must, but place them outside the kitchen proper to avoid nuisance alarms from ordinary cooking smoke.

• Purchase an easy-to-maintain smoke alarm with lithium batteries that will last for 10 years. Or have the appliances wired into the home's electrical system, eliminating the need for batteries altogether. Place an alarm outside the bedroom and on every floor of the house.

Putting Out a Fire

• Place a fire extinguisher within easy reach in the kitchen, and be sure you know how to use it. If you need to find the directions and read them before using the equipment, chances are your fire will already have burned out of control.

• Check the extinguisher periodically, according to the manufacturer's directions, to be sure it's in proper

working order. You'll be happy to know that the new generation of fire extinguishers is so well designed (I never thought I'd say this about fire extinguishers) and easy to use, you won't mind their sitting right on a countertop within easy reach.

• Install an automatic fire extinguisher in your range hood. This affordably priced product, a fire extinguisher in a small can, attaches magnetically under the hood. When a stovetop fire occurs and the flames reach the can, the extinguisher automatically releases fire-suppressing powder onto the fire.

• You can also install an automatic, but quite expensive, fire extinguisher that not only puts out a stovetop fire but also turns the electric power or gas off.

• If you're undergoing extensive remodeling and money isn't a concern, install a whole-house fire sprinkler system. It can dramatically reduce property damage and—more important— save lives.

One of the main reasons fire extinguishers were not left out in full view was because— until now—they were too unsightly and industrial. This fire extinguisher is attractive, easy to use, and right there when you need it.

Garbage & Trash

Handling garbage is an activity few of us enjoy, but an efficient system can help you handle trash and recyclables with greater ease. If you're remodeling the kitchen, consider adding pull-out waste bins—one for trash and the other for materials to be recycled. Installed under or near the sink, these bins keep garbage out of sight and also save floor space. Mounted inside the cabinet, they slide out on wire shelves or tilt out when the door is opened. Putting the bins on wheels and rolling the garbage out of the kitchen makes disposal even easier. And if your large garbage containers are also on wheels, you can roll your trash from the garage to the curb, reducing handling to a minimum. If you live in an area with pesky raccoons or other critters, look for containers with extra latches to help prevent unwanted break-ins.

Garbage disposals are very helpful in reducing the amount of food waste that might otherwise need to be carried outdoors, though in some communities building codes don't allow them. Trash compactors won't reduce the weight of materials to be disposed of, but they will reduce the volume, easing the chore of taking out the trash.

If you have a garden, consider learning how to create and maintain a compost pile; be sure to follow the rules so you get compost rather than rotten food.

Quick Fixes

Pantry

If you have a small closet in your kitchen, turn it into a pantry. Install pullout shelving hung on heavy-duty industrial tracks. Keep it stocked with staples and canned goods so that you're prepared for surprise guests or severe weather.

Flooring

Flooring that is slip-resistant and comfortable to stand on is essential in a universal kitchen. Slip-resistance is vital because grease, spills, and even wet food like lettuce leaves can cause a nasty fall. And comfort underfoot becomes even more important as we age; our knees, legs, and feet become easily fatigued while we're standing on hard surfaces. As gorgeous as tile and stone floorings are, they're tiring to stand on, and dishes break all too easily when dropped.

If your existing floor is in relatively good condition, you may be able to cover it with new slip-resistant flooring without spending a fortune. Two popular choices are vinyl and linoleum. Vinyl is plastic made from petroleum (not very eco-friendly) and comes in a wide variety of colors and patterns, including faux wood and

Wood flooring in a matte finish is a good choice for kitchens since it's safe underfoot, easy to maintain, and comes in rich natural tones.

stone. Linoleum is made primarily from linseed oil and comes in a rainbow of colors—and it's eco-friendly.

Once you've decided on the material for the flooring, choose mottled color tones that hide dirt or skid marks and a matte finish that reduces slipperiness. If replacing your kitchen flooring is not an option at this time, place a rubber or low-pile (polypropylene) mat with a beveled edge in front of the sink or work area to reduce fatigue and slips.

easy to go green
Kitchen Flooring

Green flooring is more affordable and readily available than ever before. Functional, long lasting, and beautiful too, eco-friendly flooring helps to preserve the natural environment while keeping indoor air healthy.

Here are a few of the more popular green flooring choices:

Linoleum today is attractive, healthy, and green. Made primarily from linseed oil with jute or cork backing, linoleum is available in an attractive pallet of natural pigments.

Cork is a renewable resource, has good insulating properties, is antibacterial, and is easy on knees and legs.

Wood is a beautiful, natural material and relatively easy to maintain. Choose wood from sustainably harvested forests or reclaimed from old homes and buildings.

Bamboo is a green option, especially durable. In fact, in a 2008 *Consumer Reports* test, bamboo flooring actually beat oak for durability.

Washers & Dryers

One of universal design's main goals is to make life easier; so think about moving your washer and dryer into or near the kitchen. You can cook dinner and do a load of wash at the same time! Plus, you won't have to walk up and down stairs to a basement to do the laundry.

Washers and dryers are now available in fun colors and in space-saving styles. If your washing machine is old, it's probably a water hog; now is the time to replace it with an energy-efficient model that uses up to 50 percent less water and energy per load. You'll save money in the long run.

Front-loading appliances cost more than top loaders, but they clean better and are more energy efficient, too. When shopping for a dryer, choose one with a moisture-sensor option that automatically shuts off the machine when the clothes are dry. This eco-friendly feature saves energy *and* wear and tear on your clothes. To avoid having to bend with an armful of heavy, wet clothes, go for a front-loading washer or dryer that is placed on a simple platform to make the door higher. A pullout drawer placed in the platform makes a great storage space for seldom-used items.

easy to go green
A Very Simple Fix
Here are six words that can reduce your carbon footprint: *dry your clothes on a clothesline.*

Washers and dryers on a raised platform reduce bending and reaching. You can use front-loading appliances from a seated or standing position. They are energy efficient too, using less water and electricity.

Gallery

A side-by-side refrigerator, a smooth cooktop, wall-hung ovens, and a center island sink create this kitchen's work triangle. The microwave, however, should ideally be on or below the countertop for better access and safety while moving hot foods.

This kitchen has a long countertop, making it easy to serve buffet-style meals for a large crowd. Lower the sit-down countertop to 28 to 32 inches (71 to 81 cm) if you need seating that's more accessible (and comfortable) than a kitchen stool.

In the universal kitchen, there is ample open floor space around appliances for mobility aids, which also provides generous space for two cooks.

This kitchen offers many user-friendly features that work for everyone, including multiple sinks, abundant lighting, and spacious walkways.

THE THERAPEUTIC BENEFITS of water have been celebrated for millennia. The Greeks and Romans understood the art of bathing as both a necessity and one of life's great pleasures. From medicinal baths to the joy of a deep soak, the healing powers of water to nurture and cleanse are the same today as they were in ancient times.

Instead of grand Roman baths, however, most of us are living with bathrooms designed for bare necessities, rather than enjoyment. And usually they aren't user-friendly as we age. That's why universal design is a smart choice for today's new longevity.

Whether you're remodeling an existing bathroom or just sprucing up what you have, in this chapter you'll find innovative products and stylish designs. You'll learn about bathroom essentials, like state-of-the-art bathing products and safer flooring.

And, what's perhaps more important, you'll learn how to restore pleasure to freshening up by making sure every step of the process is accessible and safe.

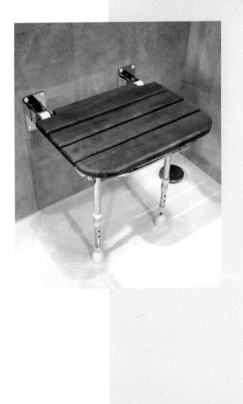

Makeovers

There are many reasons you may be considering remodeling your bathroom. Here are three common scenarios.

1. Adding a First-Floor Bathroom

If you're living in a house without a first-floor bathroom, you're thinking that some day it may be difficult or even impossible to go up and down the stairs several times a day. That's why some countries, including England and Sweden, have changed their building codes to mandate that all new homes have a bathroom on the first floor.

2. Updating Your Current Bathroom

If your existing master bathroom is cramped and unpleasant, you may want to remodel it, but you're not quite sure how to achieve a more spacious, accessible room.

3. Accommodating Your Parents

Perhaps a parent in need of care is coming to live with you for a short or extended stay. You need a wheelchair-friendly bathroom because you know that using a commode and giving bed baths are best used only as short-term strategies.

This stylish 6½ x 8½-foot (2 x 2.6 m) bathroom has an open floor plan and a curbless shower for all to enjoy. Visitors will appreciate a shower that's easy to enter and use, as will anyone who bathes the family dog! Clean lines and a soothing color scheme add to the room's spacious feeling.

Small changes can make a big difference. An easy-to-use bathroom doesn't have to be palatial: even a 6½ x 8½-foot (2 x 2.6 m) space can work nicely, especially with pocket doors and a shower-like spa. You may be able to carve out needed space by:

• Expanding a half bath by extending it into an adjacent room

• Enlarging a closet and swapping out the room's floor space for the bathroom

• Putting an addition on the house

Low-Cost Solutions

Of course, you may not be in a situation where you're able to build a new bath or even renovate an older one. You'll be relieved to know that even without remodeling, it's still possible to make many changes in your existing bathroom, without major expense, which will dramatically increase accessibility and safety. New products can be installed immediately, making the bathroom safer and easier for everyone to use.

In each of the following sections, whenever possible, I'll include both remodeling ideas and quick fixes so you can make an informed decision on which to choose to best meet your specific needs.

Accommodating a person's needs over a lifetime is an important element of universal design. You'll enjoy this handsome bathroom now and in the future for its walk-in/wheel-in shower and the vanity you can use while standing or sitting.

A transfer bench makes getting into and out of the tub easier and safer for those with limited mobility.

Bathroom Design

There are several different ways to design a smooth-functioning bathroom; where you locate the sink, toilet, and shower/bathing area depend on your available space and your mobility. Be sure to hire a designer, architect, or contractor who has experience with universal design so he or she can address your unique needs.

Here are a few guidelines to help you plan an accessible bathroom:

• Allow for an open space with a 5-foot (1.5 m) diameter to easily accommodate a scooter, a wheelchair, or a caregiver (just in case that's ever needed). Part of this space can include the open floor space under a sink or in the shower.

• If you're tight on space, provide a 3 x 5-foot (0.9 x 1.5 m) T-shaped aisle space.

• Plan a minimum clear floor space of 30 x 48 inches (76 x 122 cm) at each fixture.

A sumptuous sit-down area in a large bathroom (or bedroom) adds comfort while grooming. It's also safer to sit when putting on and taking off shoes.

Quick Fixes

Four Easy Ways to Minimize Falls

Many accidental falls take place in the bathroom. This isn't surprising when you think about the acrobatics required to climb in and out of a bathtub and the potential for falls on a wet, slippery floor. Here are four easy things you can do to reduce falls.

This highly absorbent microfiber floor mat soaks up spills from wet feet and has a safe, anti-skid backing.

1. Use a bath mat outside the tub, but only one that has an anti-skid backing. *Don't* just use a cotton towel rug: these can cause a nasty fall, because they easily slide around when walked on. If the bath mat is in the walking path, hang it up after each use.

2. Use a textured anti-slip bath mat in the tub or on the shower floor. Or you can use textured strips, as long as they're placed close together so that your foot doesn't make much contact with the tub's floor.

3. Use a bath chair if you're even a little bit unsteady on your feet. Bath chairs, now available in attractive colors from shades of blue to sunflower yellow, can add a splash of color to an all-white scheme. A brightly colored chair against a white tub is essential for anyone with low vision or dementia, both of which can create problems with depth perception.

4. Install LED night-lights in the pathway from the bed to the bathroom and also in the bathroom. Costing only pennies a year to operate, these eco-friendly lights are easy on the eyes and can help you navigate more safely at night.

Bright colors in the bathroom not only add a decorative note, but can also help a person with low vision. For example, a bath chair in a vibrant color can liven up an all-white color scheme and serve as a visual cue.

easy to go green
Materials for the Bathroom

Vanities & Cabinets. Choose formaldehyde-free particleboard or fiberboards, such as wheat-board panels. Wheat board is made from the remnants of the straw waste left over from farmers' wheat crops, milled and bound together with formaldehyde-free binders; it's very strong, exceeding the standards for particleboard in North America. Or choose woods such as bamboo that come from renewable sources, or select flooring made from recycled materials. Look for the seal from the Forest Stewardship Council (FSC).

Paint & Adhesive. Use water-based paints, primers, adhesives, and finishes with no- or low-volatile organic compounds (VOCs).

Countertops. Green laminates are available, made with recycled, formaldehyde-free materials, with low-emitting substrates; these are held together with low-VOC glues or mechanical fasteners.

Go with wood from renewable forests (for example, bamboo, Douglas fir, red alder, western maple, Oregon myrtle), or materials rescued from "deconstruction" projects.

Look for local stone.

Use terrazzo tiles, made from recycled glass.

This bathroom has plenty of open floor space and generous storage space with a sit-down vanity. The tub's side ledges allow for easy transfers, too.

Bathroom Doors

There are many types of doors on the market now that work well with universal design principles. If space is at a premium, check out pocket doors; they're an excellent solution.

Of course, you'll want a wide doorway in your bathroom (see Doors, Doorways & Hallways on page 55) to make it easy for all to come and go. And in an emergency you'll want to have two-way hinges that allow the door to swing in both directions—into the bathroom and into the room or hallway outside. This way, if you or a loved one were to fall in the bathroom and block the doorway, someone could easily get in and help. Many doorframes can be converted to two-way hinges easily, but if you have a metal one, you may need to replace the entire frame. This may be worth the effort, especially if you or a family member has a history of falls.

For safe access, install a small, swiveling metal stop on the inside of the doorframe. Set the stop so that the door opens into the bathroom; in an emergency, to open the door by having it swing *out*, swivel the metal stop out of the way and swing the door out. And make sure to choose a lock that can be opened from both sides of the door.

Pocket doors can free up valuable floor space otherwise taken up by standard swinging doors.

A wider doorway is a key universal design element because the bigger space lets every family member and guest, whether walking or rolling, enter the room.

Grab Bars

No longer the ugly ducking of bathroom design, some grab bars are now so stylish, they actually add a decorative element while improving everyone's safety and comfort. They come in a dazzling array of styles and colors and metallic finishes that match other bathroom fittings. More often than not, they look like decorative towel bars, but are built to withstand powerful forces and body weight. Choose a matte or textured finish, which tends to be less slippery to wet or soapy hands.

Installation of Grab Bars

Proper installation of grab bars is extremely important. Unless you have experience with this kind of carpentry project, I'd recommend that you hire a professional to do this job. Grab bars need to be attached:

• to wall studs (but often the studs are not located where you want to place the bar); or

• to a plywood sheet covering the entire wall (if you're remodeling); and

• with special heavy-duty fasteners, tested to withstand a 250-pound load, the requirement of most building codes.

This elegant grab bar makes bathing safer for people of all ages.

Quick Fixes

Widening Doorways

You may be able to widen the doorway without remodeling by swapping the existing hinges for "swing-clear" hinges that allow the door to swing out of the way. If you still need a little more width, remove the lower section—up to 36 inches (91.5 cm) above the floor—of the molding inside the doorframe (also called the doorstop). You'll gain as much as 3 inches (7.5 cm), depending on how the door is hung, which may be just enough to get through the doorway unscathed if you, a loved one, or a guest uses a mobility device.

For narrow doorways (I've consulted on bathrooms that had only 21-inch (53 cm) doorways)

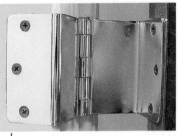

If you need only a couple more inches for a roomier doorway, swap out your old hinges for "swing-clear" hinges.

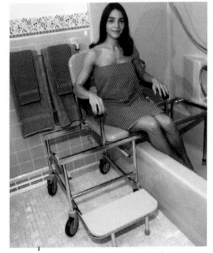

Even without remodeling, you can make your bathroom more usable with this narrow shower chair. As part of a wheelchair, it fits through doorways as narrow as 21 inches (53 cm) wide. The wheelchair seat slides into the tub along a secured track.

that can't be enlarged, consider a narrow combination wheelchair/sliding tub chair that allows you to wheel a person from the bedroom into the bathroom and, using the tub-mounted track, slide the wheelchair seat into the tub so that the chair becomes a shower chair. (These are a bit pricey, but they're significantly less expensive than a bathroom renovation; see the photo.)

If you're in a pinch, remove the door altogether (including the doorstops) and hang a beautiful drape or curtain in its place.

Avoid These Grab Bars!

There are no shortcuts with this bathroom essential. Grab bars must support a person's weight. Therefore I *don't* recommend:

Tub-mounted bars. Designed for use "only while standing," these attachable tub bars are *not* designed for use in getting up from the tub floor or even from a bath chair. These bars are designed to be used *only* with downward force while standing. They easily detach if pulled sideways (as when getting up from the tub floor or from a bath chair). In addition to interviewing the manufacturers, I tested several types of tub-mounted bars, and they all detached when used with anything other than a downward force.

Suction-cup grab bars. While they may seem miraculously strong at first, suction cups easily lose their hold and detach from the wall—and you never know when it's going to happen. The vacuum that holds them on the wall gradually weakens until it's no longer strong enough to keep the bar affixed. Also, the suction cups don't work on many types of walls, including some tiled walls.

Screwing grab bars into sheet rock is *not* adequate to support the weight of an adult, and can be even more dangerous than not having any grab bars at all. Make sure that the tile and the wall are in good condition, with no water damage that might have weakened the structure.

Grab Bar Locations for Bathing & Showering

You'll want to install grab bars in various locations, depending on your bathroom space and your personal needs. As a general guideline, consider the following locations.

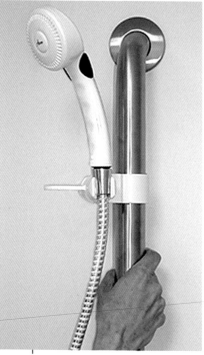

Grab bars with shower hoses attached can be dangerous—people accidently grab on to the shower hose instead of the bar. It's safer to choose a different style of shower hose.

At the Tub & Shower Entrance

You'll have a safe support to hold on to while climbing over the tub wall or entering the shower; this is a huge improvement over using the shower curtain or a slippery tile wall! A vertical bar is frequently preferred over a horizontal one because it's easier for arthritic hands to grip.

The correct position for a grab bar—whether angled, vertical, or horizontal—on a wall by the toilet is an individual choice. Horizontal grab bars are best for young adults with good upper-body strength. If you're ambulatory, you might use an angled or vertical bar positioned 1 foot (30.5 cm) in front of the toilet. New products combine toilet roll holders with hand supports.

On the Long Tub Wall

At a 45° angle, sloping up toward the showerhead, a grab bar gives a handhold when you're getting up from the bathtub floor or moving from a seated position in a bath chair to a semi-standing position when washing.

Hung horizontally, about 33 to 36 inches (84 to 91.5 cm) from the floor, a grab bar helps while standing or transferring into the tub from a seated position. If you enjoy luxuriating and relaxing with a nice tub soak, install another horizontal bar 9 inches (23 cm) above the tub for an assist when getting up and down.

By the Toilet

If your leg strength isn't Olympian, it can be challenging to rise up from the toilet, especially if a knee (or two) is bothersome. It's much easier to get up from a seated position by pushing down on supports (think of how you use armrests on chairs) *right next to you* (not on the wall). If you're remodeling, consider hinged bars that can be swung up and out of the way if and when they're not needed.

Special Needs

If you or a loved one has a condition that severely limits movement, ask your doctor for a prescription for an at-home consultation by a physical or occupational therapist. The therapist can help you choose optimal locations for grab bars.

Universal design promotes safety without sacrificing style. This fun, "wavy" grab bar complements the room's design and is a good handhold when you're moving about on a wet shower floor. When choosing an absorbent floor mat, look for one with beveled edges; they're safer.

Quick Fixes

Toilet Height

To raise the toilet to a more user-friendly height without buying a new one, you can install a hinged seat riser 3 inches (7.5 cm) high that fits *under* the existing seat. It not only raises the seat, but both the riser seat and the lid can be lifted up and down like a standard toilet seat and lid. Better yet, it doesn't significantly change the appearance of the toilet, the way the standard higher toilet seats do. Moreover, it's easily cleaned and you still get to use your existing toilet seat, but at a new height.

Toilets

While old-style toilets use up to 5 gallons per flush (GPF) or 19 liters per flush (LPF), newer models require only 1.6 GPF (6 LPF), making them a better choice for the planet's ecology. A dual-flush model saves even more because you have one type of flush for water waste (less water is used) and another for solids.

A higher toilet seat—17 or 18 inches (43 or 46 cm) high, or the height of an average chair—is a better choice if you or your guest has arthritic knees or is transferring from a wheelchair. It generally makes getting up from the toilet much easier. In the universal bathroom, the toilet is situated with open space on one side, providing room for a mobility aid or a helpful caregiver, if ever needed. A "quiet close" lid, one that slowly lowers to the seat without slamming, is another wonderful invention.

Is your toilet the right height for your needs? When seated, your knees should be level with your hips while your feet lie flat on the floor. If your toilet is too low, a higher one would give you a more ergonomic fit.

Quick Fixes

Toilets

• For an easy DIY, get a "safety" frame that attaches to the toilet. It's reasonably priced and provides side arms so you can push off (your knees will thank you). They're available only in stainless steel, but you can spray paint the frame in an attractive color to match your décor.

• To achieve an ergonomic position when rising from a seated position, some health specialists recommend installing a 12-inch (30.5 cm) vertical grab bar on the wall about 1 foot (30.5 cm) in front of the toilet, with the bottom 22 inches (56 cm) and the top 34 inches (86 cm) from the floor.

Easy to install, these side arms will help anyone who needs a little extra support getting up and down. The frames can loosen over time, so check them often to make sure they're still securely attached.

Bathroom Sinks

One of the most exciting applications of universal design for bathrooms is in the range of styles and heights of sinks. The traditional way to install a sink is at a set height of 32 inches (81 cm), regardless of the user's stature. But this height requires considerable bending for a taller person, who would find a higher position of 34 to 38 inches (86 to 96.5 cm) more ergonomic. With universal design's built-in adaptability, you can use the sink easily and ergonomically at a variety of heights, whether you're standing or sitting. For example, if you currently use the sink while standing, a universal-design installation allows you to mount the sink at a back-friendly, comfortable height now and also allows for easy lowering for use from a seated position if needed later on—without any renovation.

Adjustable-Height Sink

It's important that you install the sink into a countertop at a height that's comfortable for you now, but allows for adjustments later on. In order to minimize reaching, set the sink into the vanity or countertop as close as possible to the front edge. A built-in, adaptable vanity underneath (with removable doors and cabinet bottom, or better yet, a storage cart on wheels) gives you plenty of storage while keeping open the option of a sink height perfect for sitting.

To provide maximum flexibility so you can actually sit at the sink, select a shallow sink with a drain in the rear. Use flexible, plastic plumbing lines, available at most hardware stores, instead of rigid PVC pipes; they'll give you the option of raising or lowering the sink at some point in the future with less work.

This vanity has doors that tuck out of the way. It's a practical yet attractive design idea to accommodate a chair at the sink.

easy to go green
WaterSense Toilets

WaterSense, a program sponsored by the U.S. Environmental Protection Agency (EPA), can help you identify high-performance, water-efficient toilets that reduce your water use, save you money, and help preserve our nation's water resources. According to the EPA, toilets are by far the main source of water use in the home, accounting for nearly 30 percent of residential indoor water consumption.

The EPA reports that with new design advances, WaterSense-labeled toilets save water with no trade-off in flushing power, unlike the first-generation, "low-flow" toilets (remember flushing twice?). If every American replaced older toilets (from before 1992) with WaterSense-labeled models, each consumer would save 4,000 gallons per year, and we would save nearly 640 billion gallons of water per year, equal to more than two weeks of flow over Niagara Falls!

For more information, go to epa.gov/watersense/pubs/toilets.htm.

If you want to design the sink so that you can sit rather than stand, remember that the pipes and the underside of the sink must be insulated. You can hide unsightly plumbing behind a nice-looking panel, but be sure to attach the panel so it can be easily removed. For sitting at a sink, the proper height of the vanity is 32 to 34 inches (81 to 86 cm); legroom of 27 to 29 inches (68.5 to 73.5 cm) wide must be available under the sink. Storage capacity then can be shifted to drawers on either side of the vanity, space permitting.

Last, but definitely not least, if you can afford it, install an adjustable-height motorized sink. Yes, this is an expensive option, but if your partner is much taller or shorter than you and you would find yourselves raising or lowering the sink constantly, it may turn out to be a splurge you will appreciate for years to come. The mechanism is terrific:

any sink or countertop you select can be raised and lowered from 28 inches to 40 inches (71 cm to 101.5 cm) with the push of a button. The motor can be installed discreetly out of view under the sink. Or if you have the room, and you and your partner (or parent) have very different needs, you may find it easier to install a second sink at a different height. If the additional sink is a wall-mounted unit, it should be installed with extra-strength brackets or with extra bracing, as it can otherwise pull loose if someone leans on it.

Flexible, insulated piping and flexible-height countertops let you move the sink and countertop up and down. Storage carts on wheels complement the décor and can be easily moved to make comfortable legroom for seated users. A gooseneck faucet reduces awkward bending for taller persons, and lever faucets are easy for all to use.

This contemporary faucet is stylish and functional, and is designed to be used with only one hand.

Faucets & Handles

It's easy to add universal design to your existing sink simply by changing the faucets and handles. If you haven't looked at these products in a while, you will be pleasantly surprised that improved function can also look so good! Here are a few guidelines:

• A single-lever handle that mixes hot and cold water (as opposed to two knob handles) is a good choice, as most people—even those with arthritis—can easily use it.

• If you prefer individual hot and cold handles, use *two* lever-style handles to make running the water easier.

• Electronic faucets are an excellent choice if you want to go hands-free—and they're safer because they reduce contamination. But there are trade-offs: some models turn on when you walk by the sink—not such an eco-friendly feature. And the water temperature is usually set at an average, so you don't really get very cold or very hot water unless you make special adjustments, which are not always easy.

• If you want to reduce bending and make the sink easier to use, install the faucets near the front on one side of the sink.

This beautiful and functional sink area has two sinks, one at a taller back-friendly height and the other at a comfortable height for a seated user. The vanity doors below the sink tuck out of the way when you're sitting down to groom.

This sink overshoots the edge of the counter, which reduces the bending and reaching needed.

Lever-style handles are user friendly for everyone, as they do not require fine hand movements to operate.

This stylish and flexible sink area is good for both standing and seated use, and is tailored to the individual needs of the homeowners.

Bathtubs

If you have the space in your bathroom and love a good soak, a bathtub is a wonderful feature. Bathing can be therapeutic, helping to improve blood flow and relax sore muscles. Here are two types of bathtubs to consider for a safer soak, neither of which requires climbing over high tub walls.

1. A bathtub with a sit-down ledge reduces the chance of slipping while entering or exiting the tub. The sturdy ledge on the side of the tub gives you a place to sit while you swing your legs over the wall, slide across, and lower yourself into the water. Of course, you still need good strength and flexibility to get in and out of the tub.

2. A bathtub with a side door lets you walk into the tub over a raised lip (some are higher than others). Since you must enter the tub before it's filled and exit only after the water has been drained away, specify a quick-fill, deck-mounted faucet (it fills at twice the rate of an ordinary faucet) and a ceiling-mounted heat lamp for toasty warmth. Be aware, though, that some tub doors develop leaky gaskets; be sure to purchase one from a reputable company.

This clever redesign of the bathtub, with a side transfer ledge, makes getting in and out of the tub easier and safer—there's no tub wall to climb over. The side ledge is also a convenient spot to sit for dressing and grooming.

A walk-in bathtub with a seat means anyone can enjoy a warm, therapeutic soak, regardless of age.

Quick Fixes

A Better Bathtub
For a Deep Soak

If taking baths is one of your favorite pastimes, go ahead and splurge on an automatic bathtub seat that lowers you into the tub with a push of a button. It's both decadent and extremely safe!

For a Seated Shower
in the Bathtub

For easy entry into the tub, use a shower bench that lets you slide across the bench into the tub (see photo below) instead of climbing over the tub wall without assistance. You still have to lift your legs up and over, but this way you can do that from a safely seated position.

A variation on the shower bench is to get one with a sliding seat. You don't need to scoot across the bench; the seat itself slides over. This is ideal for anyone with delicate skin or limited movement. For safety purposes, some of the seats have a lock that keeps the seat in place while you're showering or getting on and off the bench.

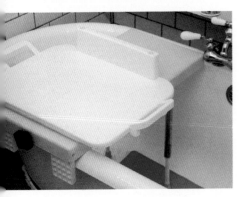

Accessible Showers

The universal home includes a walk-in/wheel-in shower that welcomes all users to its rejuvenating benefits. There are many styles, ranging from traditional to contemporary. If you make only one remodeling change in your current bathroom to make it safe for aging in place, install one of these showers. Everyone in your family will love it! Presented next are two types of accessible showers.

This shower is inviting to both standing and seated users. When planning an accessible shower, keep in mind that a 5-foot (1.5 m) turning radius allows a wheelchair user to exit without having to back in or out.

Spa Treatment

A spa-like shower creates a spacious and open layout in which the shower isn't completely separate from the rest of the room. The floor (usually tile) is sloped to carry the water to the drain. A shower spa design eliminates the cost of purchasing a shower unit and also does away with a frequent tripping hazard in the bathroom, the 2-inch (5 cm) lip along the bottom of a conventional shower unit. You can hang a curtain for privacy. Be sure the curtain is on a bar that's bolted into the ceiling. If you happen to slip and grab the curtain, you want to be certain the curtain rod holds your weight.

Prefab Choices

A prefab shower unit is another solution. The smallest size recommended is 42 x 60 inches (about 1 x 1.5 m). The larger the shower size, the easier it is for a caregiver to help. It's a good idea to purchase a curbless, walk-in roll-in model. Be sure to select a shower unit sized to fit through your existing doors, or buy a unit that comes in sections to be reassembled on site. Some come equipped with fold-up seats, grab bars, and an anti-scald shower control, all of which are highly desirable.

IT'S WISE TO BE SAFE

Shower Drains
The slope to the drain must be designed correctly or you'll have problems with flooding. Also, talk to your architect or contractor about the best type and number of drains. For example, do you need one or two round drains, or would one long trough-like drain handle the water better?

This serene, light-filled shower has multiple showerheads, a built-in folding bench, grab bars, and a gently sloped center drain. Small matte-finish tiles provide good traction.

Prefab showers come in many sizes, including units that fit into an existing bathtub space. They do not come with collapsible dams to prevent flooding, but you can purchase this dam separately and have it installed.

You have myriad choices when it comes to shower controls. You can match all your hardware—shower controls, faucets, towel bars, and even grab bars—for a seamless, integrated look.

If you buy a curbless shower unit less than 42 inches (106.5 cm) wide, consider installing a rubber, vinyl, or foam collapsible threshold—½ to 1 inch (1.5 to 2.5 cm) high—that compacts when rolled or walked on. This way, you can easily roll over the threshold with a wheeled device, and the threshold will still keep water from spilling onto the bathroom floor. You'll need to replace these dams periodically because they deteriorate over time; but keep in mind that any shower lip can be a trip hazard, even a collapsible one.

Faucets for Showers & Bathtubs

As is true with the hardware for sinks, there's an incredible range of styles available for faucets and showerheads. For easy access, mount the tub spout and the shower controls near the entry.

Install a low-flow showerhead. Until recently, a typical showerhead delivered about 5 to 8 gallons per minute (GPM)—or 19 to 30 liters per minute (LPM)—while the current standard for low-flow heads is about 2.5 GPM (9.5 LPM).

A large, soft-grip, ergonomic handle makes this handheld shower easier to use.

IT'S WISE TO BE SAFE

Swap out your old faucets and showerheads with ones that have built-in anti-scald controls. They will protect everyone from hot water surges and other causes of preventable scalding.

Prevent Scalding

Thinner skin, decreased sensitivity to heat, slower reaction time, and certain medical conditions—especially neuromuscular, neurological, and cardiovascular disorders—put older adults at high risk for scald burns. But the good news is that most burns can be prevented.

There are several types of anti-scald valves. The size of your home and your individual needs determine which one is best. Here are a few pointers, but it's wise to discuss with your plumber what's best for your situation.

Whole house. If you own your home, it's more efficient to install a scald valve at the water heater to serve the entire house. Using anti-scald valves allows water in the water heater tank to be kept at higher temperatures. This reduces the risk of Legionnaires' disease bacteria (which are killed in very hot water temperatures) and delivers the tap water at lower, safer temperatures.

By room or by location (plumber installed). If you're remodeling, choose a shower with an anti-scald temperature control and an adjustable high-temperature limit that lets *you* set the maximum water temperature. This way, the water always flows at a safe, constant temperature. If water temperatures aren't kept consistent, you could get a sudden burst of hot or cold water when a toilet is flushed or the dishwasher or washing machine is turned on.

DIY devices. You can install anti-scald devices only where you need them. They automatically reduce scalding water to a trickle when it reaches a set temperature, and then turn it back on when you remix the water to a safer temperature. You can buy a fixed showerhead, a handheld shower unit, or a tub spout that already contains an anti-scald sensor. Or you can purchase a screw-on anti-scald valve that can be installed on your existing showerhead or faucet.

A handheld shower unit is a good universal design choice. It comes equipped with a large handle for easy holding and is ideal for people who prefer to shower while seated. The same unit can also be mounted on a 2 to 3-foot (61 to 91.5 cm) vertical track on which you can easily move the showerhead up or down. Some units have a built-in anti-scald feature.

Digital temperature controls allow you to customize the water temperature for safe, comfortable bathing. Also helpful are a handheld showerhead and an easy-to-reach tub drain.

This faucet handle has an integrated hand support. When choosing grab bars or hand supports for the bathing area, look for matte finishes; wet, soapy hands can easily slip on polished surfaces.

Lighting

Good bathroom lighting is a critical element of universal design and independent living. It helps us see better when we put on makeup, brush our teeth, change our contact lenses, etc. It can make a small bathroom seem more spacious, help you see better at night, and even make the room warmer. Depending on your bathroom's size, there are several types of lighting to choose from:

• A ceiling fixture provides good general lighting.

• A ceiling-mounted heat lamp can take the chill out of the air and is an inexpensive luxury for any age.

Twin sconces with fabric shades illuminate this sink area with soft, easy-on-the-eyes light, as there are no exposed bulbs or glass covers.

IT'S WISE TO BE SAFE

Electrical Precautions

Be sure your electrician puts in outlets that are ground fault interrupted (GFI) so that the risk of shock is completely eliminated. And as a final safety precaution, set up a telephone near the bathtub, just in case someone needs to call for help and can't get up, especially if you or a loved one has a history of falls.

• A wall-mounted vanity light above the mirror, shedding light upward and downward, works well. Design features include an opaque front, acrylic lens on the bottom, an open top, and eco-friendly fluorescent tubes.

• Wall-mounted vanity lights (no exposed bulbs, please) on both sides of the mirror help light the face (important for grooming) and add a decorative element.

• A recessed, waterproof ceiling light provides good illumination for the bathing area.

• Eco-friendly LED night-lights, which cost only pennies a year to operate, are available in most home stores in easy-on-the-eyes blue or green colors.

Longevity Essentials

Keeping Warm

Did you know that the body's thermo regulators don't work as effectively as they did when we were younger? And after a shower or bath, you can become unpleasantly chilled faster than you expect.

Here are a few ideas to help you keep warm and cozy:

• Use a plush robe (terry cloth or fleece) after bathing.

• If you're remodeling the bathroom, look into a radiant heated floor to warm up the floor (and your feet). Learn more about radiant flooring on page 174.

• Install a ceiling heat lamp.

When planning your bathroom, consider the electrical needs for both lighting and room temperature. For example, radiant electric flooring transforms cold tile and stone floors into warm and toasty surfaces while also helping to heat the room.

Ventilation

Windows and good ventilation make a bathroom more comfortable and healthier. The floors will be less slippery, and mold will be less likely to develop. I recommend installing a ceiling vent and an exhaust fan; be sure to install them on a separate switch from the overhead light. There are new "quiet fans" with a barely noticeable noise, while others sound as if a jet plane is taking off in your bathroom! Ask for a sound demonstration of the model before you purchase it.

A glass block wall offers a modicum of privacy while allowing natural light to flood the room. Fresh air and ventilation from the window help reduce indoor pollutants.

Floors

In the universal home, flooring materials are easy to walk or wheel on, don't contribute to indoor pollution, and have a matte, nonpolished finish. And for bathrooms, due to the presence of steam and water, you'll want the least slippery flooring. Slipperiness is technically measured by the "coefficient of friction" or COF. A high COF, 0.6 or higher is generally a safe, slip-resistant floor.

Regardless of your flooring choice, keep in mind that lighter-colored floors make spaces seem larger—a real plus in a small bathroom.

Radiant Flooring

Stepping barefoot on a warm bathroom floor is very comforting. You can enjoy this experience if you install a radiant heated floor. If you're remodeling, think about adding an electric radiant heating system for the bathroom only. (The expensive alternative is a hydronic system for the whole house; a pump circulates hot water through tubing in the floor.) An electric system consists of thin heating cables, like the wires in a heating pad, installed under the flooring. Some easy-to-install systems have a heating cable woven into an adhesive-backed fiberglass mesh.

Electric radiant heating is most effective with ceramic tile, because the tile itself conducts and stores heat, but radiant heating can also be used with other floor coverings, including linoleum. Always check with the radiant heating manufacturer about alternative flooring; you may need a more powerful unit for surfaces other than tile.

For energy efficiency, connect the system to a programmable thermostat, so that the floor is heated only when needed—for example, from 6:00 to 8:00 A.M. and again from 8:00 to 10:00 P.M.

The creative possibilities within universal design can also enable you to function at your best. This clever bathroom has a shower area that's actually part of the room. The whirlpool tub has a tub surround that makes transferring easier. The no-threshold entryway with small matte flooring tiles is safe for everyone.

Popular Flooring Choices

Bathroom flooring is available in a wide range of styles and materials. The following are all universal design in terms of safety.

• Sheet resilient flooring, like vinyl or linoleum, is a wise choice: it's easily cleaned and softer and warmer underfoot than ceramic tile or stone. Choose a nonwax, matte, slip-resistant finish to help protect against falls.

• Ceramic tile, made primarily from clay fired at very high temperatures, is another popular bathroom choice. The beauty of ceramic tile is the dazzling array or colors, sizes, and textures, in addition to its functionality: it's durable, waterproof, and easy to maintain (as long as the grout lines are done right). Choose a ceramic tile in a textured, matte, slip-resistant finish specifically rated for bathroom flooring.

• Mosaic tiles, made from porcelain or ceramic, are a classic choice for bathroom floors. They're ideal for showers too, as their small size, 1 to 2 inches (2.5 to 5 cm), allows for flexibility in following the contours of the sloped floor to the drain. These small tiles have more grout lines, which may increase slip resistance. Mosaic tiles are available in many colors and patterns in pre-mounted plastic mesh sheets for easy installation.

• Stone flooring. Marble, granite, slate, and limestone can add a luxurious tone to the bathroom's look and feel, but be sure to specify a textured, *non-slip* finish (honed or sandblasted), as polished stone floors resemble an ice-skating rink when wet. Stone flooring is definitely a splurge item, but if you have a healthy budget, include a radiant heating system to keep the cold stone floor warm underneath bare feet.

• Carpeting. For those who prefer carpeting for its warmth and softness underfoot, its sound-absorbing qualities, and its slip protection, your best bet is to use commercial carpeting with a dense, low pile, an anti-microbial treatment, and waterproof backing. To distinguish this type of carpeting from regular carpeting, ask for it by its trade name: Resilient Textile Sheet Flooring. Regular carpeting in the bathroom may promote the growth of mold, retain odors, and will need to be replaced more frequently. An alternative: use carpet tile—the type with dense pile and antimicrobial treatment—that allows you to replace individual tiles as necessary. But keep in mind that moisture may raise the corners on these tiles, which can make for an unsafe walking surface.

Small mosaic tiles are a good choice for the shower area. A no-threshold entryway reduces tripping and other hassles during entrance and exit.

Gallery

A walk-in bathtub with a low entry curb is much easier to use than one with a high wall you have to step over. This beautiful bathing area features matte-finish linoleum, and an inviting seat to use while grooming.

This calm and soothing bathing area includes a bathtub with a wooden surround for easy entry, windows for light, fresh air, and healthy ventilation, and a sink designed for accessibility and support.

CHAPTER 9

Livable Communities

IN ADDITION TO EXPERIENCING SANCTUARY AND INDEPENDENCE in a home that has universal design features, we also can enhance our well being through our relationships with friends, family, and community. We're social animals by nature; we need each other as much as we need light and air. There are also times when we have to depend on other people for all kinds of vital services.

Like a universal home, a "livable" community is one that people of all ages can enjoy, a place that encourages participation and increases our quality of life. A livable community has resources to help us meet a variety of needs so we can remain as independent as possible while staying connected to those around us. And at some point, if we desire even more companionship or need medical care, a livable community has viable housing options so we can remain in our own town, close to friends and family.

In this chapter, you'll learn about essential community features that contribute to healthy longevity, and explore how communities across the United States are creating age-friendly neighborhoods the universal way.

Key Services in Livable Communities

A livable community features a range of services and amenities: from grocery stores to health services to cultural institutions to outdoor parks. In addition, services such as home repair, meal deliveries, and home health care can enable you (or an older parent) to care for yourself at home. Some communities offer these services à la carte while others provide a one-stop shopping service, where for a membership fee, you can make a single phone call and the organization's staff does all the rest.

Let's first take a look at two key services: transportation and à la carte home maintenance.

Getting Around— Transportation

Even if you can now hop into a car and take care of all your needs, what if you could no longer drive? Could you still easily visit with friends, enjoy a show, buy groceries, or see your doctor? Accessible transportation options are key to keeping you connected with the social life in your community.

Individuals without transportation options are less satisfied with their communities—and their lives.

A livable community provides a range of transportation services to help you get around, from accessible taxis, buses, and trains to more specialized services, like private cars and vans at reduced fares. To learn what's available in your community, search AARP's website (aarp.org) for its State-by-State Guide to Transportation Assistance, or check with your local transportation authority.

A livable community offers opportunities for intergenerational activities that enrich our lives and connect us to our families and to each other.

creating**fellowship**

Key Features of a Livable Community

• Affordable and appropriate housing for people of all ages and income levels

• Safe, well-designed sidewalks that connect people to services and activity centers

• Roads designed for safe driving with clear signage, traffic stops, and pedestrian crosswalks

• Safe and convenient transportation options, including access to public transportation

• Community services such as grocery stores and other retail, plus health services (hospital, clinic, or outpatient services)

• Access to recreation, leisure, and cultural activities

• Places to participate in public meetings and events

• Well-run community centers, parks, and recreation centers

• Security and safety

• Opportunities to become a volunteer and give back to the community

Keep Up with Your Driving Skills

Of course, many of us older adults still drive—and drive well! On the other hand, you or a family member may need to brush up on your skills. AARP offers a Drivers Safety Program designed for drivers ages 50+ who want training in the latest techniques on driving safely. Offered both online and in locations throughout the country, the course covers topics such as defensive driving, new traffic laws, and rules of the road. You'll also learn how to adjust your driving to allow for age-related changes. The course is available to AARP members and non-members, and as an added bonus—many insurance companies give discounts on car insurance after you've completed the class. For information about classroom or online courses, call toll-free at 1-888-AARPNOW (1-888-227-7669) or visit aarp.org/drive.

À La Carte Home Maintenance Services

Maintaining a home can be a daunting task at any age, but at "advanced ages" (whatever age that might be for you), it's best to delegate climbing a ladder or repairing cracks in the walkway to someone else. You may already have good relationships with handymen and women you know and rely on, but if not, it's comforting to know a trusted resource that can help you out. Check to see if your community has small businesses, community organizations, or local religious groups who employ dependable service professionals such as:

• Handymen/women for minor home repairs or tasks, such as hanging storm windows and cleaning downspouts and gutters.

• Licensed professionals for electrical or plumbing work.

• Housekeepers for everyday cleaning or for a major spring cleanup.

Longevity Essentials

Companionship Is Heart-Healthy

Loneliness and the lack of emotional and social support can leave you vulnerable to heart problems, according to research led by Dr. Dara H. Sorkin at the University of California, Irvine.

Researchers asked 180 men and women, ranging in age from 58 to 90, to rate their level of loneliness, as well as the availability and number of individuals they can turn to for support or companionship. For every unit increase in loneliness, there was a threefold increase in the odds of being diagnosed with a heart condition. Having just one person around for emotional support seemed to be enough to reduce the risk of heart disease; however, it took relationships with several individuals to realize the health benefits of social support.

—November 2002, *Annals of Behavioral Medicine*

A livable community has a variety of transportation options, including public transportation, accessible vans, and bicycle lanes.

Longevity Essentials

Social Ties Are Good for Your Brain

There's mounting evidence that an active social life may help keep your memory sharper. Research by the Harvard School of Public Health shows that older adults with active social lives have a slower rate of memory decline. Researchers collected data over a six-year period on almost 17,000 Americans age 50 and older, who participated in the Health and Retirement Study. They found that individuals who were the most socially integrated (assessed by marital status, volunteer activities, and frequency of contact with children and neighbors) had less than half the rate of memory decline compared with those who were the least socially integrated. "Social participation and integration have profound effects on health and well-being of people during their lifetimes," said Dr. Lisa Berkman, senior author.

—July 2008, *American Journal of Public Health*

Five key lifestyle factors help promote a healthier, happier longevity: *lifelong learning, strong friendships, lower stress, physical activity,* and *good nutrition.*

Communal Living: Variations on a Theme

As growing numbers of boomers begin reaching that "certain age," more and more of them are thinking outside the box and creating new paradigms for sharing the hearth. And for good reason. Companionship and shared living can be comforting to the heart and, especially in our current economic climate, good for our bank accounts. Sharing living space with friends or like-minded individuals who share your lifestyle, values, and outlook on life can help you age with greater vigor and comfort.

Companionship is welcome at any age, but can be a great source of comfort in our later years. As seen here, enjoying a meal with good friends and neighbors is one of life's greatest pleasures.

More women are exploring the concept of sharing their homes with younger persons who help out around the house in exchange for free or reduced rent.

Sharing Your Home

For some individuals, having a companion who also helps out around the house enables them to remain in their own home. There are communities that already offer a service to help people find a suitable companion. For example, the South Burlington-based HomeShare Vermont will match up a student or someone else who works outside of the home with an older adult who wants extra help with chores. Companions can either work approximately 12 to 15 hours per week (doing chores, shopping, cooking, etc.) in exchange for free rent, or they can work less and pay reduced rent. To learn more, visit homesharevermont.org. If you're interested in such a service for yourself or for a parent, you can also check with eldercare.gov to see if a similar organization exists in your community.

Female Households

If you're of the female persuasion, you should know that women frequently age alone in large houses that they're reluctant to leave. In the not-too-distant future, I think we'll see more female households with several friends living together, offering each other companionship, fun, and a helping hand when needed.

If your home is spacious and can be easily modernized with universal design features, starting your own intentional household may be your next great adventure. Or you and your housemates may decide to purchase a new space—whether it's a large loft in New York City or an old farmhouse in Vermont—and remodel it, using universal design principles. By the way, you'll have greater harmony if each person has her own bedroom and shares other areas of the house. And of course, you'll want a few "house rules," such as who does the housekeeping. Better yet, if your budgets allow, pool your resources and hire someone. You can also decide which nights of the week you'll dine solo and on which nights you'll enjoy each other's cooking and company!

Longevity Essentials

Walkable & Exercise-Friendly Communities

Physical inactivity is a risk factor for the leading chronic disease deaths in the United States today: heart disease, cancer, stroke, and diabetes. The more walking and exercise opportunities your community offers, the more likely you are to get the exercise you need. A walkable and exercise-friendly community has:

• Sidewalks with curb cuts

• Parks with walkable trails

• Exercise classes tailored for the 50+ crowd (aerobics, weights, and stretching)

• Gyms or malls (or other alternative indoor spaces) for inclement weather

• Bike paths

Exercise is key for healthy longevity. A livable community is one that has options for both indoor and outdoor exercise, such as tennis courts, accessible walking paths, and indoor yoga and stretch classes.

Virtual Assisted Living—in Your Own Home

Assisted living was all the rage in the 1990s, when a move to this type of residence gave a person easy access to vital programs and services. But for those of us who want to remain in our own homes, "virtual" assisted living offers the next great opportunities. You get all the benefits and services of assisted living, whether you go to town or the town comes to you, at less cost than if you were to reside in an assisted-living residence.

Although each virtual assisted-living organization is unique, becoming a member generally entitles you to a variety of services. For an annual membership fee that's put toward the cost of services, you make just one phone call and receive the service you need from an approved vendor list. Depending on the virtual assisted-living community, services may include transportation for shopping, doctor's appointments, or to a local park. You

Virtual assisted living services are cropping up all over the United States for individuals living at home who desire some of the benefits of community living. Members get entrée to special events, like group dining or trips to local museums, and priority access to needed services, like transportation, home maintenance, and daily wellness calls.

Virtual assisted living allows you to remain in the comfort of your own home and receive a range of services. A yearly membership fee includes services like transportation and group outings. Home care and maintenance chores can also be arranged, often at a lower rate.

can choose from various social, educational, and cultural events, including group dining at favorite restaurants, discussions with community leaders, and trips to concerts and museums. And if you need a plumber, a nurse, or an aide, the organization will arrange for that too—often at a discounted rate. A daily wellness telephone call gives you the peace of mind that comes from knowing that someone is watching over you.

If your community seems like a good candidate for a virtual assisted-living organization, contact Boston's Beacon Hill Village, a successful pioneer in the field, for advice on getting started. For a fee, the Village staff will send you a copy of the Beacon Hill Village Founder's Manual, a "how-to" guide that includes information about what worked and what didn't, as well as gives practical advice about which services are likely to be the most

popular (refer to the link at beaconhillvillage.org/building.html).

To learn more about how you can be part of the grassroots efforts to make your community a livable community, go to aarp.org and search for Livable Communities for up-to-date information.

New Models of Livable Communities— Cohousing at 55+

The opportunity to share expenses, the sense of security that comes when someone is present in the event of difficulty, the availability of companionship through long, cold winter months: these advantages have encouraged many older adults to consider some sort of shared living arrangement. While many of us are familiar with the more popular types of shared living—such as the larger, developer-driven active adult communities or assisted-living residences—the newer models are smaller, lifestyle-driven, and run and developed by the people who live there.

Originating in Denmark some 35 years ago, cohousing began as intentionally built small-scale neighborhoods (20 to 40 households) comprised of people of all ages. Individual homes are usually clustered around a courtyard, giving everyone more opportunities to interact with neighbors. People have their own homes (attached or single family), but share a large common house with a kitchen, dining room, and recreational spaces. Community members divide chores and take turns cooking meals, which are shared together two or three times a week.

Although this model works well for many people, it may not be adequate to support successful aging in place, which requires communities to furnish more than shared resources and close connections with neighbors. In addition, certain services need to be readily available and communities must be accessible. Enter cohousing with a twist—for people age 55+. In this model, wellness options and amenities may include healthy diets, exercise, and separate quarters for a nurse or home health aide (or at least space put aside for future needs).

Cohousing Resources for People Age 55+

Here are some organizations to check out for more information about this type of living arrangement:

• **The Cohousing Association of the United States**, Bothell, Washington: cohousing.org or 866-758-3942.

• **Elder Cohousing Network**, Boulder, Colorado: eldercohousing.org or 303-413-8066

easy to go green
Eco-Friendly Communities

If you're looking for a community that uses sustainable building practices, here are some key features to look for:

• Recycled or local building materials and furnishings

• Healthy indoor air quality

• Energy-efficient appliances

• Water and energy conservation

Access to the outdoors is a vital element of healthy longevity. Choose a community that has accessible sidewalks and pathways that connect homes with common areas and neighbors.

Some Very Good Questions

If you're contemplating living in an existing cohousing community or starting one from scratch, here are a few questions to ask:

1. Is the community a good match for your values and lifestyle? You'll want to do your homework to see which community is the best fit for you. Some communities are more spiritually oriented; others more interested in lifelong learning or the arts.

2. Is the community accessible? A community that's built the universal way gives you more opportunities to age in place. For example, if the cohousing community you're interested in has two-story homes, check to see that they have:

• A no-step entrance (or one that can be easily adapted)

• Interior stairs that can be retrofitted with an electric stair chair, closets stacked one on top of the other to accommodate an elevator if needed, and/or a downstairs that can be adapted to handle a master bedroom

• An accessible bathroom

• Wide (32- to 36-inch [81 to 91.5 cm]) doorways

• Wide (42-inch [106.5 cm]) hallways

• Shared community spaces that are accessible

3. How close is the community to goods and services? Even if you can drive at present, you don't want to be automobile-dependent. Some communities, like Wolf Creek Lodge in Grass Valley, California, are within walking distance to trails, grocery stores, banks, and restaurants. If goods and services are farther away, make sure the community offers transportation services.

At Silver Sage Co-Housing Village, the common house includes exercise and meditation rooms, as well as a large kitchen and dining area for community meals. There is an elevator for easy access to the second floor communal spaces and condos.

Staying connected with others is essential for a happy, long life. People who have strong friendships have fewer physical limitations because they live more active lives. They also maintain their mental facilities and approach life's difficulties with a more positive attitude than people who are isolated.

4. What happens if someone becomes very ill? If you're without a partner, or have a partner who's ill, it can be comforting to know neighbors are nearby when you need a helping hand. In some communities, when a member becomes sick, the community draws up a "care plan" that assigns neighbors to drive the individual to doctor's appointments, bring over hot meals, or just stop by to check that everything's OK. Communities differ in terms of how much help is offered or how long someone can remain if the community can't properly meet his or her needs.

As an example, ElderSpirit—a cohousing community in Abingdon, Virginia, that's committed to spiritual growth and caring for each other—has a written statement that acknowledges that at

some point, members may need institutional care. But when that time comes, the community designates a member to stay in touch with the person—easing the transition and keeping the individual connected to the ElderSpirit community even after he or she has moved to a facility.

Starting Your Own Community

It can be very appealing to live with people you know and care about and with whom you share similar values. That's why groups of friends are joining forces and building their own cohousing communities. You'll have more control over the look and feel of the neighborhood; with the help of an architect, you can plan your own universally designed community. It takes a lot of time and commitment to develop a cohousing community, but the rewards can be worth it.

Longevity Essentials

Assisted Living and Nursing Homes

Although assisted living and nursing home residences are beyond the scope of this book, these facilities are being increasingly designed or retrofitted with universal design features and wellness programs that allow their residents to live more fulfilling lifestyles. If you are looking for a long-term care residence for a loved one, however, there are important care considerations to investigate. See AARP's Caregiving Checklists for evaluating an assisted living or nursing home residence at www.aarp.org.

CHAPTER 10

From Plan to Reality

MAKE THIS THE YEAR to get your home in shape. You know that to live long and well, you need a comfortable, user-friendly home. Perhaps you've been dreaming about adding a spacious walk-in shower, a beautiful first-floor bedroom, or an accessible backyard deck for family get-togethers.

I'll help you think through whether it makes sense to upgrade your current home for healthy aging in place, or whether the right decision is to move to a home that already has universal design features.

In this chapter I'll show you how to make your dream a reality by setting priorities, developing a master plan, finding a contractor, and avoiding the many pitfalls and unnecessary costs of remodeling. I'll help you navigate the renovation process, the universal way. You'll learn about some basic financing strategies, too.

Stay or Move?

Although most people 50+ want to stay in their own homes, not all houses are suitable for an entire lifetime. Choosing a brand new, universally designed home may turn out to be the best way to have the independent lifestyle you wish to maintain. For a better quality of life, consider moving if:

• You can't easily remodel your home for accessibility. For example, there are too many stairs, or the house has small, cramped rooms and narrow hallways.

• Your community isn't a "livable" one. For instance, it doesn't have adequate access to quality health care, transportation, and other vital services, such as home maintenance.

If you live in an easily adaptable home *and* in a livable community, but you're still undecided about whether to stay or move, incorporating the features of universal design into any remodeling projects is still a wise choice—for both your future and your pocketbook. The more changes you make, the more usable your home will be over a lifetime and, because it will attract a wider group of buyers, the greater its resale value should you decide to sell.

A universal designed home allows people to maintain a healthy lifestyle as needs change. This handsome remodeled kitchen serves the homeowners well while they remain active, but it will also help them function independently as they age.

Getting Started

It's smart to have a master plan for the design features you'll need for an active, full life—regardless of your age. Review your completed checklist from chapter 2 (you *did* fill this out, didn't you?). It will provide you with a clear picture of where your house is on the universal design spectrum, and therefore what it will take to make small and possibly large changes. Depending on your immediate needs and budget, you may want to make the changes in stages or all at once. It's a good idea to remodel your home when you're healthy and able to do so with less pressure or anxiety. Planning ahead gives you peace of mind: you'll know that in the event of a health or other family crisis, you or a loved one can continue to live in your own home to the fullest extent possible.

You'll also need a plan for financing the changes (see Financing Strategies, page 198). You may find that some dreams are beyond your financial capabilities, while others are less costly than you think. Once you have an idea of what you'd like to do, you may need an architect to design the job, as well as a general contractor to hire and supervise all the tradespeople. The scope of the work will determine your requirements, and a professional can analyze the cost of the renovations you're considering. It's best if the people you're working with have experience with universal design remodeling.

List by Priority

First, make a prioritized list of the goals you want to achieve. Keep in mind the three key design elements I mentioned in chapter 2:

1. An accessible no-step entrance

2. An accessible bedroom (it could be a converted den on the first floor)

3. An accessible bathroom

Your list might include such changes as: swap the first floor bathtub for a prefab walk-in shower unit; add a small ramp from the garage to the back door; replace the round doorknobs with lever-style handles. Depending on your budget, you may also be considering larger renovations. Maybe you want to widen all the doorways or make the kitchen compatible for cooks and company of all ages and physical abilities. Or perhaps you already have a first-floor bedroom but would like to add a private patio off it so you can look at your garden. Put numbers 1, 2, and 3 on your list of "Must Haves," and everything else on "Nice to Have." Prioritize!

When creating a master plan, consider how to make your home better serve your long-term needs. Even if you are fully mobile now, it's smart to plan for the future and think about features you may want to add now that will assist you in the future. Options include consolidating your living space to one floor or installing a stair climber, a wheelchair lift (shown here behind the half door), or an elevator. The small handrail offers safe support for a person with balance problems.

A level entryway that permits wheelchairs and walkers to pass through easily is an important universal design element.

List by Location

Now it's time to get very specific. Use the checklist from chapter 2 to organize the improvements your house needs by room and location. For example, Indoor Stairs: add handrails on both sides; add rocker-style light switches at top and bottom. Outdoor Stairs: install electrical outlet for safe low-voltage lighting.

List by Trade

Make a separate list organizing the improvements by trade, and list them in order of importance; for instance, if you need electrical work done, list everything an electrician needs to do, regardless of whether it's in the kitchen, bathroom, or another room. Do the same for the plumbing and carpentry. For big projects, you're probably better off delegating the entire hiring process to a qualified contractor (see Choosing Professionals to Work With, page 193). If it's a small project and you're acting as your own contractor, hire the tradesperson you need for the items at the top of your list first. That way, you'll have accomplished the most important tasks, even if you don't get all the way through the list right away.

List by Purchases to Make

Draw up a list of all the purchases you'll need to make on your own. Locate a home supply store that has a wide selection, so you can purchase as many items as possible in one place. However, some items may need to be specially ordered.

Consider all the electrical upgrades that will make your home safer and more accessible, like GFIC outlets in all wet areas and easy to use rocker light switches installed at a convenient height.

This small bathroom was reconfigured to include a no-threshold shower design and efficient storage space.

Choosing Professionals to Work With

If you've never undertaken a major renovation or built your own home, don't worry: you don't have to live out the nightmares of others who have. Good planning and careful decision-making, especially when hiring professionals, can help you avoid "construction job trauma."

Not every designer or contractor is well versed in universal design, or in the critical construction techniques that can eliminate or minimize housekeeping and, what's more important, injuries. For example, a curbless walk-in shower needs a sloping floor, but not just any old sloping floor will do. The degree and direction

of the slope is critical, or flooding occurs. Mopping up after each shower is not only a nuisance: wet, slippery floors can be dangerous. In addition, if contractors are not familiar with the new, stylish universal design products on the market, they may recommend more institutional-looking products.

Organizations that list professionals with universal design credentials can be good sources for referrals to architects, designers, and contractors. These include the American Society of Interior Designers, the American Institute of Architects, and the National Association of Home Builders (NAHB). The NAHB is one

of the founders of the Certified Aging-in-Place Specialists (CAPS) training program, which teaches professionals how to remodel the universal way to create aesthetically pleasing *and* accessible environments. Visit www.aarp.org and you'll find a link to a page where you can locate a CAPS graduate near where you live. Other tried-and-true sources are friends and family, as well as the staff at local home-improvement stores; sometimes these stores train employees to be knowledgeable in universal design, and sometimes they maintain a list of tradespeople they recommend.

On-going communication with your contractor will help your project stay on course and on budget, especially if you have a detailed, well thought-out contract.

10 Tips for Working with a Contractor

The following 10 tips will help you avoid the many pitfalls and unnecessary costs of remodeling, and keep headaches to a minimum. They'll also help you communicate better and maintain a good working relationship with your contractor.

1. Verify the Contractor's License

Find out if your state or local jurisdiction requires a contractor to be licensed or registered (36 states do). One way to check this out is to visit the Contractor's Reference License Site at contractors-license.org, or call your local state license board. If your jurisdiction requires licenses, ask to see the contractor's and make sure it's not expired.

2. Check References

Talk to several past clients and ask the following questions:

• Did the contractor show up for work on a regular basis?

• Did the contractor finish the job in a timely manner?

• Did he or she clean up the construction site at the end of each day's work?

• Did he or she return calls to discuss any problem areas?

• What were the contractor's greatest strengths?

• What were the contractor's greatest shortcomings?

3. Check for Any Complaints

Call your local Better Business Bureau or your state's office of consumer affairs, and see if anyone has registered a complaint against the contractor.

Make sure you really like the paint colors you are purchasing by testing small swatches on the walls, and looking at the colors in different lighting situations.

4. Get Bids from Different Contractors and Compare Prices

Obtain at least three written bids if possible; contractors do not charge for bids. But the quality of the items in a bid can account for a substantial difference in price, and you must be certain that you're comparing apples to apples. Be sure each contractor has identical plans and specifications. If there is a major discrepancy between the bids, you need to discover the reason. The lowest bid is not necessarily the one to jump at.

IT'S WISE TO BE SAFE

Environmental Hazards

Before you drive a nail or sign a contract, check for lead, asbestos, and black mold. You don't want to endanger yourself, the workers, or your chances for future resale. For more information on minimizing exposure during remodeling to mold and mildew, asbestos, lead paint, pollutants in new building products, check out the Environmental Protection Agency website, epa.gov/iaq/homes/hip-concerns. You'll find a number of informative articles on this subject.

5. Check the Contractor's Insurance Coverage

He or she should have liability coverage for both property damage and for personal liability. Insufficient insurance coverage may compromise your contractor's ability to obtain local building permits. It may also leave you liable in the event of some mishap.

6. Obtain a Detailed Written Contract

Most renovation headaches arise when too much is left open to interpretation; if the contract isn't specific enough, you'll run into problems. You want every purchase clearly detailed, as well as firm start and completion dates. Be sure the contract states that all construction practices and techniques will conform to local building codes and standards.

7. Make the Contractor Responsible for Obtaining Building Permits

This is a time-consuming but essential process for which your contractor should be responsible.

8. Agree to a Reasonable Payment Schedule

The customary fee schedule is one-third in advance, one-third halfway through the job, and one-third upon completion. Never pay the entire fee up front, and never pay the balance before the job is finished to your satisfaction and has passed any required inspections. Don't make changes in your plans without a written estimate of the associated cost, and remember that every change costs money.

9. Include a "Broom Clean and Debris Removal" Clause

Be sure the contract specifies that the contractor must leave the working area "broom clean" every night—but consider hiring a housecleaner for a thorough job at the end. The contractor should also be responsible for removal of all construction debris.

10. Include a Method of Conflict Resolution in the Contract

Arbitration and mediation are often better choices than litigation, and they bring resolution faster and at less expense for both parties. If a conflict with your contractor does develop, it's a good idea to state your position in writing and keep copies of your correspondence.

Whether your renovation is large or small, include in your contract that the working areas must be swept clean each night. To get a thorough cleaning at the end of the project, however, you'll need to give it a good scrub yourself or hire someone to do it.

Surviving Renovation in Style

A Special Word to Renters

If you're like most people, you may think you can't renovate a rental apartment beyond hammering in a few picture nails or sprucing up the walls with a fresh coat of paint. The good news is that you can make changes to your living space, and federal law is on your side. The downside is that you'll probably have to pay for it yourself.

The Fair Housing Act states that landlords must not refuse tenants the opportunity to make "reasonable" modifications if they're prepared to absorb the cost of the changes. Here are a few examples of "reasonable" modifications:

• Installing grab bars in the bathroom

• Widening doorways

• Installing wheel-in showers

• Lowering countertops

Your landlord, however, is entitled to ask for a description of the proposed modifications, proof that they will be done in a professional manner, and evidence that all the necessary building permits, if needed, will be obtained.

If you plan to modify the apartment in a way that would affect a future tenant's ability to use the space (such as replacing the bathtub with a walk-in/roll-in shower), the landlord *may* require you to pay the estimated cost for the restoration into an escrow account. For more information, contact your local Center for Independent Living, a national advocacy group expert in housing issues and legal rights (www.virtualcil.net/cils).

Very few of us have the option of checking into a luxury hotel while our home is being renovated. But just in case the paint fumes get the better of you or something unexpected happens, like a new toilet doesn't work, it's wise to line up a friend or family member with whom you could stay. Living in a house during remodeling requires considerable patience, a tolerance for chaos (or at least confusion), and an extraordinary sense of humor. If you think you're qualified on all three counts, you'll probably survive to tell the story, especially if you follow the advice offered here.

Set Yourself Up in Another Room

The most important strategy is to camp out in an area that's outside the construction zone, and move every single thing you need into this one area. If you're redoing your kitchen, you'll need to set up a temporary one, furnished with a hot plate, microwave, and a small refrigerator—and keep the telephone numbers of your favorite take-out restaurants handy!

Keep the Place Clean

A plastic sheet hung from ceiling to floor and taped down during construction will minimize plaster dust. Decide with the contractor in advance where he or she will store tools at day's end, and make sure the contractor agrees the site will be at least broom clean when the crew leaves.

Define the Work Hours

For your peace of mind, and that of others if you live in an apartment, set a reasonable starting hour for the workpeople in the morning and a definite time when construction ends each day.

If you are renovating your bathroom, you may be able to remove an adjacent closet or use a few feet from an adjacent room to create a more spacious and accessible bathroom.

easy to go green
Specifying Green Materials

Going green won't change the look of your home. But it will improve energy efficiency and air quality, and it won't break your bank account. Some green products cost more, but many are now priced the same or only slightly more than standard products. That's because green is going mainstream. Make sure to specify energy-efficient products with brand names (and colors where applicable) and include these in the requirements you give the contractor.

Supervise

There's no question that you'll be inconvenienced during construction, but being on-site will help you supervise and notice errors as they occur. Second-guessing the contractor every hour of every day, however, does nothing to improve your working relationship, but it's fair to ask reasonable questions periodically, especially if you notice work that you think is inconsistent with your design.

Consider a Temporary Home for Your Pets

Construction dust and noise can be difficult for anyone to live with, and pets are no exception. Plus, with workers going in and out of your house, you don't want the additional worry of losing your four-legged friends through an inadvertently open door while you're busy with other matters. Find a temporary home (a nearby kennel or good friend) to help them get through the worst of the demolition or construction phase.

Keep the Big Picture in Mind

It's easy to get lost in the day-to-day stress and lose perspective of the big picture when you're in the middle of a renovation. Remind yourself *often* of what's down the road—a safer, healthier life in a more user-friendly, accessible home. That's a goal worth striving for.

During a renovation, you may need to find a temporary home for your pets to shield them from daily work upheavals, like noise and construction dust.

This unusual mudroom/bathroom with a utility sink is a good place to wash dishes while your kitchen is being remodeled.

Financing Strategies, Tax Deductions & Credits

You'll need to evaluate your financing options as you plan your makeover, so you know how large a project your budget can handle and the types of finishes, appliances, and furnishings you can afford. In this section, I'll highlight a few financial strategies, including using your own funds or assets wisely, some borrowing options, as well as government and private funding. And lastly, I'll review important tax deductions that you won't want to miss out on, including medical expenses (if you qualify) and green credits.

Using Your Own Funds Wisely

If you have sufficient savings or investments you can liquidate, the decisions are comparatively easy; ask your financial adviser which investments in your portfolio are the most logi-

Surviving "construction job trauma" can be challenging, but keep your eye on the goal and you'll find the hassle is worth it. If you're opening up small spaces by removing walls, widening doorways, and adding more lighting, remind yourself of how you're investing in a healthier longevity.

cal candidates for sale. Home-equity loans can be good sources of financing if you have adequate equity built up and can easily make the monthly re-payments. They're less costly overall than reverse mortgages, but you have to begin paying them back shortly af-ter taking them out.

Using Your Home Asset Without Monthly Payments —Reverse Mortgages

If your primary financial asset is your home, and if you're at least 62 years old, you may want to consider a "reverse mortgage," also known as a "home equity conversion loan," as a way to access the equity in your property in order to pay for a renova-tion. Assuming that you've fully paid for your residence or have only a small mortgage, it's usually possible to borrow part of the value in your home, even if you have no income or a poor credit history. Before you get too far into planning how to spend the money, make sure that this is the right financial strategy and the right time to borrow against the equity in your home. There may be better and less expensive ways to finance your renovation.

A major drawback to reverse mortgages is their high upfront fees, which can run into several thousands of dollars, depending on the value of your home. Reverse mortgages are available in many forms from many institutions, so be sure to shop around for the best fees, interest rates, and terms and conditions. You may want to seek help from a finan-cial advisor to choose the best option for you. And, as always, be cautious when choosing which financial insti-tution to deal with.

Home equity loans or reverse mortgages can be sources of financing for renovating your home and making it accessible. Talk to a financial planner beforehand for advice on your situation, as each option has pros and cons.

Most reverse mortgages are feder-ally insured so that if the lender expe-riences financial difficulties, you'll not be affected. It's best to find a federally insured loan where possible, for other reasons as well: lending standards, consumer disclosures and other pro-tections that are required, and poten-tially lower interest rates.

Usually under a reverse mortgage there are no required loan repayments until the last borrower dies, sells the house, or moves permanently. At that time, you or your heirs will have to repay the loan, typically from the pro-ceeds of the home sale. It's comforting to remember that with reverse-mort-gages, you're still the owner—able to sell when you choose and make any cosmetic or structural changes you want (though you can't rent out your home). In most cases, reverse mort-gages are "non-recourse loans," mean-ing that you or your heirs will not owe more than the sales price of the home, even if the sale of the house doesn't cover the entire balance of the loan.

For more information that can help you decide if a reverse mortgage is right for you, see AARP's website at aarp.org/revmort.

Private Grants & Government Funding

If you need help financing your reno-vations, a thorough search for funding should be a priority at the beginning of your project; it usually takes some digging around to find these valuable resources. Depending on the health of our national and local economies, states and individual communities may have funding from local organizations and government programs that can help pay for needed renovations.

Private Grants

Be sure to inquire at organizations like Habitat for Humanity and your chapter of the National Multiple Sclerosis Society. (Visit nationalmssociety.org; on the homepage, you'll find a link at the top to a chapter locator.) Talk with local churches and other religious groups, which often help build home ramps. If you're a veteran, the VA may be a valuable resource. When you call any group, don't be shy—just explain your situation and ask if they can refer you to another group if they can't provide help themselves.

Government Funding

Most government funding is channeled through individual states, so you need to explore your state's unique funding and programs. Some states are funding universal design remodeling for eligible individuals who choose to receive care in their

When planning a renovation, think of both the large-scale and small-scale changes that will help you lead a safer and more active lifestyle. For example, well-anchored rails along the edge of a countertop can support individuals with balance or mobility issues.

Many organizations train youth to build ramps at no or little cost to help older people remain in their homes.

homes instead of in nursing homes. For example, New York's Access at Home program pays for widened doorways, accessible bathrooms and kitchens, and other features that enable independent living.

The best place to start searching for information on local resources is the Eldercare Locator, a free service of the U.S. Administration on Aging. There you can find out about all government programs in your state, including Medicaid. Call 1-800-677-1116 or visit their website at www.eldercare.gov. And don't forget that we live in an age in which Google has made more information available than ever before in the history of the world, so you may want to use this as part of your resource tool kit!

Tax Deductions

Yes, Virginia, there are certain tax deductions available. Read on to find out if you're situation is described.

Medical Expenses

Many improvements or modifications made to your home can be deducted as medical expenses if their purpose is to provide medical care for you, your spouse, a parent, or a dependent. Many of the modifications discussed in this book are fully deductible as medical expenses, including:

- Installing ramps

- Adding porch lifts

- Widening doorways or hallways

- Modifying stairs or installing an elevator

- Adding grab bars or handrails (for any room)

- Lowering kitchen cabinets

- Modifying smoke and fire alarm systems

- Modifying entrance and exit doorways

- Grading the ground to provide access

The IRS does not regard these modifications as increasing the value of a home and the costs are treated as medical expenses. Keep in mind that you can only deduct medical expenses to the extent that they exceed 7.5 percent of your adjusted gross income (Form 1040, line 38). For this reason, you may prefer to bunch qualified home improvements into one year. Be sure to talk to your tax adviser or accountant when you're in the process of planning these deductions.

Other improvements, which the IRS *would* regard as increasing the value of your home—such as adding an extra bedroom for someone who is disabled—are treated differently. In these cases, the cost of the improvement must be reduced by the increase in the value of the home to calculate how much is deductible. For you non-accountants, this just means that the deduction is lowered by the amount that the home value increases. (Cost of improvement minus increase in home value = medical deduction.)

Whether you're in your 50s or 80s, a universal design home with an accessible entry will contribute to beautiful and safe living in the second half of your life.

For more information, see IRS Publication 502, "Medical and Dental Expenses." All IRS publications are downloadable at www.IRS.gov/formspub, or you can call 1-800-829-3676 to request a publication. For answers to questions, you can call the IRS at 1-800-829-1040.

Green Tax Credits

If you're remodeling your home and want to go green, there are tax credits available for certain energy-efficient changes. For instance, tax credits at 30 percent of the cost

First-floor living, with a convenient eat-in kitchen and an accessible bedroom and bathroom, encourages safe, healthy living.

Quick Fixes

Tax Credit vs. Tax Deduction

A tax *credit* directly reduces the tax you owe, while a tax *deduction* only reduces the amount on which you pay taxes; so if you owe $1,000 and get a $300 credit, you only owe $700. That's money in your pocket from Uncle Sam.

Now is the time to explore a new world in which opportunities replace barriers and friendships blossom in a more accommodating home and community.

are available for energy-efficient changes to doors and windows, insulation, roofs, and water heaters. But the total credit for these items cannot exceed $1,500.

The even better news is that for certain other kinds of modifications, tax credits at 30 percent of the cost have *no* upper limit and are available through 2016. These modifications include geothermal heat pumps, solar panels, solar water heaters, small wind-energy systems, and fuel cells. Clearly, these are more expensive items, but if you're serious about going green and the government is willing to pay 30 percent of the cost, by all means, forge ahead!

You can get more information at energystar.gov/taxcredits.

A New Frontier

This book was written to show you how a universally designed home can contribute to beautiful living for everyone, regardless of age or physical ability. Features like no step entryways, spacious bathrooms, and accessible backyards make life easier for you, your family members, and guests. Planning and following through on universal design changes to your home can be a time as exciting as when you bought your first home: you can bring that same enthusiasm and hopefulness to universal design that you brought to that first home. Universal design creates a new way to live, allowing everyone to realize their full potential.

I hope this book has provided you with useful information and has inspired you to engage actively in adapting your home for a long, healthy life.

About the Author

Rosemary Bakker holds a master of science in gerontology and is a certified interior designer. She is a Research Associate in Gerontologic Design in Medicine at the Weill Cornell Medical College in New York City. Rosemary is also the director of ThisCaringHome.org, an award-winning multimedia website on home safety and design for caregivers of persons with dementia. She has consulted with numerous individuals and companies and has made presentations on design and healthy longevity to diverse audiences, ranging from interior designers and housing experts to consumers, health care professionals, and Fortune 500 corporations. Rosemary was a guest on Martha Stewart Living Radio; has appeared on CBS, NBC, and PBS; and was featured in the Public Lives column of the New York Times and in AARP The Magazine. She lives in New York City with her husband, Jonathan. She can be reached at RosemaryBakker.com.

Acknowledgments

To my editor Deborah Morgenthal, for her warmth and wisdom in helping me craft the book and for encouraging me to find my voice.

To AARP, an organization that understands the individual and social importance of making our homes universally accessible for a lifetime.

To H.D., for believing in me.

To the faculty and staff at the Division of Geriatrics, Weill Cornell Medical College, who supported my advocacy of the role of the built environment in healthy longevity.

To my best friend and husband Jonathan, who was there for me each step of the way; I simply could not have written this book without his love and support. It was our great shared adventure.

To others too innumerable to mention who have contributed to the book, I am deeply grateful.

Resources and Photo Credits

Organizations

AARP
888-687-2277
aarp.org
Photos on pages 10, 14, 21 (middle), 24 (top), 29, 39 (bottom), 50 (right), 51, 67, 71 (top), 125 (middle), 126 (bottom), 138 (left), 140 (bottom), 142, 148 (top), 161 (middle right), 164 (top), 165, 167 (left), 179, 180, 182 (right), 189 (top), 192 (top), 193 courtesy of AARP

AbleData (government product database)
800-227-0216
abledata.com

The American Institute of Architects
800-AIA-3837
aia.org

Center for Universal Design
College of Design
North Carolina State University
919-515-3082
design.ncsu.edu/cud

Cohousing Association of the United States
866-758-3942
cohousing.org

Concrete Change
404-378-7455
concretechange.org
Photos on pages 66 (top), 201 (top) courtesy of Concrete Change

Eldercare Locator (local resources)
800-677-1116
eldercare.gov

ENERGY STAR
888-782-7937 Hotline
energystar.gov

Habitat for Humanity ReStores (home improvement/furnishing second hand stores)
habitat.org/env/restores.aspx

IRS
Medical and Dental Deductions
800-829-3676
IRS.gov/formspub

Lighting Research Center
Rensselaer Polytechnic Institute
518-687-7174
lrc.rpi.edu
Photo on page 111 (left) courtesy of the Lighting Research Center of Rensselaer Polytechnic Institute

National Association of Home Builders
800-368-5242
nahb.org

National Institutes on Aging
800-222-2225
nia.nih.gov

National Shared Housing Resource Center
nationalsharedhousing.org

Queensland Department of Public Works
Smart and Sustainable Homes Program
07-32244961
sustainable-homes.org.au

Photos on pages 15, 64 (bottom) courtesy of Stockland, Sustainable Home Doonella Noosa, part of the Queensland Department of Public Works, Smart and Sustainable Homes Program

Universal Design Alliance
770-667-4591
universaldesign.org
All photos courtesy of Universal Design Alliance; photo on page 37; designed by Carol Axford of CDA Design Group; photography by Fred Gerlich Photography

Photo on page 52 (left); designed by Bernice R. Phelps of Defining Spaces; photography by Fred Gerlich Photography

Photo on page 53; designed by Shannon Schilling of Design Details; photography by Fred Gerlich Photography;

Photo on page 72; designed by Holly B. Peck of Holly Peck Interiors; photography by Fred Gerlich Photography

Photo on page 84; designed by Anna Marie Hendry of Classic Interiors by Anna Marie; photography by Fred Gerlich Photography

Photo on page 85; designed by Anna Marie Hendry of Classic Interiors by Anna Marie; photography by Fred Gerlich Photography

Photo on page 105 (top); designed by Kathleen Pyrce of Pyrce Williams Design Group; photography by Fred Gerlich Photography

Photo on page 105 (bottom); designed by Ann Wisniewski of AJW Designs, Inc.; photography by Fred Gerlich Photography

Photo on page 120; designed by Margery Caruana Farr of Margery Farr Design; photography by Fred Gerlich Photography

Photo on page 125 (top and bottom); designed by Pamela Goldstein Sanchez of Pamela Sanchez Designs and Fusion Design Group, LLC; photography by Fred Gerlich Photography

Photo on page 134; designed by Margery Caruana Farr of Margery Farr Design; photography by Fred Gerlich Photography

Photo on page 143 (left); designed by Pamela Goldstein Sanchez of Pamela Sanchez Designs and Fusion Design Group, LLC; photography by Fred Gerlich Photography

Photo on page 144; designed by Pamela Goldstein Sanchez of Pamela Sanchez Designs and Fusion Design Group, LLC; photography by Fred Gerlich Photography

Photo on page 151; designed by Candace McNair of Bright Ideas Interior Design, Inc.; photography by Fred Gerlich Photography

Photo on page 159; designed by Pamela Goldstein Sanchez of Pamela Sanchez Designs and Fusion Design Group, LLC; photography by Fred Gerlich Photography

Photo on page 167 (top right); designed by Lisa Brooks of Living Spaces Studio; photography by Fred Gerlich Photography

Photo on page 169 (right); designed by Lisa Brooks of Living Spaces Studio; photography by Fred Gerlich Photography

Photo on page 170 (bottom); designed by Lisa Brooks of Living Spaces Studio; photography by Fred Gerlich Photography

Photo on page 173; designed by Lisa Brooks of Living Spaces Studio; photography by Fred Gerlich Photography

Photo on page 176; designed by Lisa Brooks of Living Spaces Studio; photography by Fred Gerlich Photography

Photo on page 189 (middle); designed by Pamela Goldstein Sanchez of Pamela Sanchez Designs and Fusion Design Group, LLC; photography by Fred Gerlich Photography

Weill Cornell Medical College
ThisCaringHome.org (a home safety project of Weill Cornell Medical College for dementia caregivers)

Green Guides
Products and Home Energy Saving Ideas

American Council for an Energy Efficient Economy
aceee.org

Green Seal
greenseal.org

US Department of Energy
energy.gov

US Green Building Council
greenhomeguide.org

Architectural Firms

Brennan + Company Architects
410-788-2289
brennanarch.com
Photos on pages 60, 77 (right) courtesy of Brennan + Company Architects; photography © Anne Gummerson Photography

röm architecture studio
206-545-7336
romarchitecture.com
Photos on pages 17 (bottom), 31 (top), 33 (right), 61 (bottom), 63 (top), 135, 155 (middle), 166 (top), 200 (left): design © röm architecture studio; photography © Dale Lang, 2008

Samsel Architects
828-253-1124
samselarchitects.com
Photos on pages 61 (top), 73 (bottom), 129 (top) courtesy of Samsel Architects

Designers/Builders

Kathy Adcock-Smith, ASID, RID
Adcock-Smith Design
214-956-8020
adcock-smithdesign.com
Photo on page 147 courtesy of Adcock-Smith Design; photography by Jan Marie Davis

Rosemary Bakker
rosemarybakker.com
Photos on pages 13 (top), 31 (bottom), 33 (left), 42 (left), 66 (bottom right), 87, 90, 112 (bottom), 117, 149, 158 (bottom left), 166 (bottom), 171 (top left), 192 (left) courtesy of Rosemary Bakker

Blue Professional Interior Design Services
614-487-9870
bluedesigns4u.com
Photo on page 122 (top) courtesy of Blue Professional Interior Design Services

CG&S Design-Build
512-444-1580
cgsdb.com
Photos on pages 40, 55 (left), 95 (top), 97 (left), 98 (left), 100, 127 (right), 128 (top) courtesy of CG&S Design; photography © Greg Hursley/ttlmgt.com

Dakota Builders, Inc.
520-792-0438
dakotabuildersinc.com
Photos on pages 172 (top left), 175 (bottom) courtesy of Dakota Builders, Inc., Tucson; photography by Karen Danhood

Greeson & Fast Design
828-252-0400
greesonandfast.com
Photo on page 177 (top) courtesy of Greeson & Fast Design

Harrell Remodeling
650-230-2900
harrell-remodeling.com
Photo on back cover (top) and photos on pages 74, 97 (right) courtesy of Harrell Remodeling and Emerald Light Photography

Heartland Builders, LLC
888-445-6503
heartlandbuildersllc.com
Photos on pages 26, 56 (top) courtesy of Heartland Builders, LLC

Kaléh and Associates, Inc.
310-289-9746
kalehdesign.com
Photos on pages 56 (bottom), 111 (right) courtesy of Kaléh and Associates, Inc.

Louis Tenenbaum, LLC (consultant)
Independent Living Strategist
301-983-0131
louistenenbaum.com
Photo on page 200 (top) courtesy of Louis Tenenbaum

Post & Beam Design/Build
410-515-6464
pbdesignbuild.com
Photos on pages 11, 22, 27 (top), 32 (top), 36, 38, 59 (right), 109 (left), 146, 160 (top), 174 courtesy of Post & Beam Design/Build

Universal Designers & Consultants, Inc.
(consultant)
301-270-2470
universaldesign.com
Photos on pages 131, 190, 197 (bottom) courtesy of Universal Designers & Consultants, Inc.

Mike Vowels, Universal Design Consultant
425-765-7165
universalandgreen.com
Photo on page 189 (bottom) courtesy of Michael Vowels

Randall Whitehead (lighting consultant)
415-626-1277
randallwhitehead.com
Photos on pages 71 (bottom), 89, 95 (bottom), 106: lighting design by Randall Whitehead; interior design by Nancy Satterberg; photography by Dennis Anderson

Manufacturers
Electrical
Advanced Lumonics, LLC (LED lighting)
877-855-1625
earthled.com
Photo on page 45 (top) courtesy of Advanced Lumonics/EarthLED.com

Heath/Zenith (lighting controls, motion activated for table lamps)
800-858-8501
Photo on page 42 (left) courtesy of Heath/Zenith

Home Automation, Inc. (home control products)
504-736-9810
homeauto.com
Photo on page 108 courtesy of Home Automation, Inc.

JASCO Products Company (lighting)
405-302-2426
jascoproducts.com
Photos on pages 41 (bottom), 42 (right) courtesy of JASCO Products Company

Bathroom
American Valve, Inc. (anti-scald fixtures)
678-684-1150
americanvalve.com
Photo on page 171 (lower left) courtesy of American Valve/HotStop

Eagle Health Supplies, Inc. (bath transfer benches, sliding seat)
714-532-1777
eaglehealth.com

Great Grabz (grab bars)
239-403-4722
greatgrabz.com
Photo on page 127 (left), 139, courtesy of Great Grabz; photography by Brynn Bruijn Photography
Photo on page 155 (top), 163 courtesy of Great Grabz; photography by Thomas Minion Photography

MABIS DMI Healthcare
(bath transfer benches, sliding seat)
800-526-4753
mabisdmi.com

Moen Home Care (grab bars & other products)
800-882-0116
homecare.moen.com
Photos on pages 32 (left), 157 (bottom), 161 (lower left), 164 (bottom), 171 (right) courtesy of Moen Home Care

Patent Marketing, LLC
(transfer bench with sliding seat)
800-455-3101
versabath.com
Pictured on page 169 (lower left).

R.D. Equipment
(chair on wheels with sliding seat and track)
508-362-7498
rdequipment.com
Photos on pages 161 (middle) courtesy of R.D. Equipment

Safety Tubs (walk-in tubs)
877-304-2800
safetytubs.com
Walk-in tub images on pages 168 (bottom) provided by Safety Tubs, the leader in walk-in tub technology

Shower Solutions USA
(collapsible shower thresholds)
407-314-2176
showersolutionsusa.com

Sisus Corporation
(chair on wheels with sliding seat and track)
877-828-6699
sisuscorp.com

Kitchen
AD-AS (motorized height adjustable systems: sinks, countertops, and cabinets)
800-957-2720
ad-as.com

GelPro (anti-fatigue, non-slip mats)
866-GEL-MATS (435-6287)
gelpro.com
Photo on page 19 (left) courtesy of GelPro

Guardian Safety Solutions International, Inc. (automatic stove turnoff)
800-786-2178
www.guardianssi.com
www.guardyourkitchen.com

Home Depot (fire extinguisher)
Home Hero fire extinguisher, page 149

Pioneering Technology Corporation
(Safe-T-element)
800-433-6026
pioneeringtech.com
Photo of Safe-T-element on page 136 (top) courtesy of Pioneering Technology Corporation

Rev-A-Shelf, LLC
800-626-1126
rev-a-shelf.com
Photos on page 148 (bottom) courtesy of Rev-A-Shelf, LLC

Universal Design Products (height adjustable sinks, countertops, and cabinets)
877-811-7511
universal-design-products.com

Williams-Pyro, Inc. (automatic range hood extinguisher)
817-872-1500
www.stovetopfirestop.com

Bedroom
EasyClosets.com
800-910-0129
www.EasyClosets.com
Photos on pages 118, 119 courtesy of EasyClosets, LLC

Wall Bed Systems, Inc.
419-738-5207
wallbedsystems.com
Photos on pages 34, 35, 105 (middle) courtesy of Wall Bed Systems, Inc.

Interior
Herman Miller, Inc. (office chairs)
888-443-4357
hermanmiller.com
Photo on page 99 courtesy of Herman Miller, Inc.

Kolbe & Kolbe Millwork Co., Inc.
(windows & doors)
715-842-5666
kolbe-kolbe.com
Photos on pages 70 (right) courtesy of Kolbe & Kolbe Millwork Co., Inc.

Pella Corporation (windows)
800-374-4758
pella.com
Photos on pages 41 (top), 47 (top), 48 courtesy of Pella Corporation

Uplift Technologies, Inc.
(lift & light solutions)
800-387-0896
up-lift.com
Photo on page 88 courtesy of Uplift Technologies, Inc.

Exterior

Backyard America (decks, ramps, lighting)
703-392-5152 x102
backyardamerica.com
Photo on page 68 (left) courtesy of Backyard America

J. Dabne Peeples (custom landscaping)
864-859-6570
thecollinsgroup.org
Photos on pages 75 (top, middle), 76 (bottom), 78 courtesy of J. Dabne Peeples

Prairie View Industries, Inc. (access ramps)
800-554-7267
pviramps.com
Photos on pages 25 (top), 64 (top) courtesy of Prairie View Industries, Inc.

Amy Wagenfeld (landscaping & gardens)
Therapeutic and Developmental Design Specialist
617-875-4883
Photo on page 81 (bottom) courtesy of Amy Wagenfeld

Personal Aids

Bean Products, Inc.
(ergonomic bed reading pillow)
800-726-8365
beanproducts.com
Photo on page 112 (top) courtesy of Bean Products, Inc.

Drive Medical (mobility aids & more)
516-998-4600
drivemedical.com
Photo on page 158 (lower right) courtesy of Drive Medical

Dynamic Living, Inc. (general products)
888-940-0605
dynamic-living.com
Photos on pages 17 (top), 39 (middle), 58, 88 (bottom), 155 (bottom), 161 (top right), 162 (left) printed with permission from Dynamic-Living.com

GrandCares (smart home monitoring technology)
262-338-6147
grandcare.com

Healthcraft Products (bath accessories)
813-885-5244
healthcraft.com
Photos on pages 162 (right), 172 (bottom left) courtesy of Healthcraft Products

Hertz Supply (beds & bedroom furnishings)
800-321-4240
hertzsupply.com
Photo on page 122 (bottom) courtesy of Hertz Supply

Savaria Concord Lifts, Inc. (elevators & lifts)
800-661-5112
savariaconcord.com
Photo on page 52 (right) courtesy of Savaria Concord Lifts, Inc.

Photographers

Andrea Rugg Photography
612-827-1004
andrearugg.com
Photos on pages 57 (bottom), 73 (top), 83 (bottom), 96, 130 (top), 133 (left), 152 (bottom), 172 (right) © Andrea Rugg Photography.com

Chris Usher Photography
703-739-4346
www.chrisusher.com
Photos on pages 160 (bottom), 185 © Chris Usher Photography

Collinstock Architectural Imagery
612-735-7717
collinstock.com
Photos on pages 57 (right): interiors by In-Unison, Minneapolis; architecture by Choice Wood, Minneapolis; photography by Andrea Rugg/Collinstock
Photos on pages 73 (top): design/build by Keith Waters and Associates; photography by Andrea Rugg/Collinstock

Dale Christopher Lang
206-293-6075
nwphoto.net
Photo on back cover (bottom) and photos on pages 13 (middle), 54 (bottom), 57 (top), 63 (bottom), 116, 188, 197 (top), 202 © Dale Lang

Emerald Light Photography
503-559-4551
emeraldlight.com
Photos on pages 3 (bottom), 6 (bottom), 27 (bottom), 102, 104, 154, 156, 157 (top), 192 (lower right) © emeraldlight.com

Greg Hadley Photography
703-425-5671
greghadleyphotography.com
Front cover photo and photos on pages 12, 18 (bottom), 20, 30, 43, 46, 47 (bottom), 66 (left), 82, 98 (right), 124, 126 (top), 132, 136 (bottom), 138 (right), 141, 145, 152 (top), 153 © Greg Hadley Photography

Jay L. Clendenin
207-828-8787 x300
Auroraphotos.com
Photos on pages 3 (top), 5, 21 (bottom), 183 (top) © Jay L. Clendenin/Aurora Photos

Jessie Walker Associates LLC
847-835-0522
jessiewalker.com
Photos on pages 24 (bottom), 54 (top), 63 (middle), 68 (right), 91, 103 (right), 123 (top), 168 (top)
© Jessie Walker

Philip Wegener Photography & Video
303-444-8414
philipwegener.com
Photos on pages 13 (bottom), 28, 32 (bottom right), 44 (right), 129 (bottom), 130 (bottom), 191 © philipwegener.com

Rhonda Chen, CID
Interior Design Details
714-990-8083
richen@sbcglobal.net
Photo on page 170 (top)

Roe Osborn Photography
774-237-0051
roeosbornphoto.com
Photo on page 177 (bottom) by Roe A. Osborn

Scot Zimmerman Photography
800-279-2757
scotzimmermanphotography.com
Photo on back flap and photos on pages 39 (top), 55 (right), 65 (top), 72 (top), 83 (middle), 109 (right), 137, 150, 158 (top), 167 (bottom) © Scot Zimmerman

Shutterstock.com
Photos on inside front flap and on pages 6 (top), 8, 9, 16, 19 (right), 21 (middle), 23, 25 (bottom), 49, 50 (left), 62, 65 (bottom), 70 (left), 75 (bottom), 76 (top, right), 77 (left), 81 (top), 83 (top), 86, 88 (left), 92, 93, 94, 101, 107, 110, 123 (bottom),133 (right), 134 (left), 140 (top), 143 (right), 178, 181,182 (left), 183 (right), 184, 187, 194, 195, 201 (bottom) Used under license from shutterstock.com

Steve Mann Black Box Photography
828-236-9777
blackboxstudio.com
Photos on page 18 (top), 59 (left), 69, 79, 80, 113, 114, 115, 121, 196 by Steve Mann, photo © Lark Books, a Division of Sterling Publishing, Co., Inc.

Warner Photography, Inc.
828-254-0346
warnerphotography.com
Photo on page 128 (bottom) © Warner Photography, Inc.

WikiMedia Commons
commons.wikimedia.org
Photos on pages 44 (left), 45 (bottom) courtesy of WikiMedia Commons

Special Thanks

Jonathan Bakker
Photos on pages 31 (bottom), 42 (left), 66 (bottom right), 87, 90, 112 (bottom), 117, 149, 158 (lower left), 169 (lower left), 202 (author) courtesy of Jonathan Bakker

Chinese Acupuncture & Herbology Clinic
Asheville, NC

David's Bedrooms & Mattresses
828-670-1116
davidsbedrooms.com

Peira Dermody
peira.vitadesign@gmail.com
Photos on pages 13 (top), 33 (left), 166 (left), 171 (top), 192 (lower left) courtesy of Peira Dermody

Tom & Melinda Henderson
Asheville, NC

Bobby J. Wiggins
Asheville, NC

Wonderland Hill Development Company
(building communities)
303-449-3232
whdc.com
Photo on page 186 courtesy of Wonderland Hill Development Company

Keep Learning and Experiencing

More Great Titles From AARP

available from Barnes & Noble and booksellers everywhere

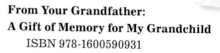

Live & Learn: Expressive Drawing:
A Practical Guide to Freeing the Artist Within
ISBN 978-1600592812

Many people may long to draw—but feel too intimidated to try. Written by arts educator Steven Aimone, this book is packed with solid, friendly, hands-on instruction, as well as inspiring images, and backed by the trusted AARP name. Aimone teaches an accessible style called expressive drawing that emphasizes line and mark, rather than rendering a specific object. Exercises start off simple and quick, encouraging readers to work on instinct and feeling, while the later ones focus on detail and refinement.

From Your Grandfather:
A Gift of Memory for My Grandchild
ISBN 978-1600590931

For My Grandchild:
A Grandmother's Gift of Memory
ISBN 978-1402723254

Share your wisdom and experience, bring family history alive, and celebrate the full life you lead now in these one-of-a-kind keepsake volumes. With questions and conversational prompts written from a grandchild's point of view these special journals include spaces for recording thoughts and pasting in photos and mementos.

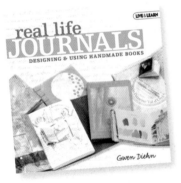

Live & Learn: Real Life Journals
Designing & Using Handmade Books
ISBN 978-1600594922

Whether you want to record your travels, jot down daily thoughts, try a new hobby, or explore changes in your life, journals can enrich the experience. From a flexible notebook you can roll up and slip into your back pocket to an elegant, satin-covered book filled with watercolor paper, this second book in AARP's Live & Learn series will show you how to design and create a custom-made journal that will both inspire you and enhance the experience you're documenting. You'll also find a gallery of journals and profiles of journal-makers to spark your own creativity.

Conversations with My Father:
A Keepsake Journal for Celebrating a Lifetime of Stories
ISBN 978-1600590894

Conversations with My Mother:
A Keepsake Journal for Celebrating a Lifetime of Stories
ISBN 978-1600590887

These beautiful keepsake volumes are the perfect place to record an aging parent's milestones and recollections while opening up ongoing dialogue. You'll find engaging questions to ask that will encourage your mother or father to provide facts about aspects of their lives and relate rich details about their experiences. There's space for you to record their answers as well as to include some of the photos and mementos that illustrate them.

Index